# VEGAN CHOCOLATE TREATS

100 easy dairy-free, gluten-free
and refined-sugar-free recipes

—

# VEGAN
# CHOCOLATE
# TREATS

*Emma Hollingsworth*
*Kyle Books*

**An Hachette UK Company**
www.hachette.co.uk

First published in Great Britain in 2023
by **Kyle Books, an imprint of Octopus
Publishing Group Limited**
Carmelite House
50 Victoria Embankment
London EC4Y 0DZ
**www.kylebooks.co.uk**

ISBN: 9781914239564

Distributed in the US by Hachette Book Group,
1290 Avenue of the Americas,
4th and 5th Floors, New York, NY 10104

Distributed in Canada
by Canadian Manda Group, 664 Annette St.,
Toronto, Ontario, Canada M6S 2C8

Publisher **Joanna Copestick**
Project Editor **Samhita Foria**
Photographer **Jen Rich**
Design **Helen Bratby**
Food styling **Kathy Kordalis**
Props styling **Max Robinson**
Production **Allison Gonsalves**

A Cataloguing in Publication record for this
title is available from the British Library

Printed and bound in **China**

*For my three little chocoholics, Azaria,
Buddy and Boaz, and my beloved Mr H*

**CONTENTS**

# INTRODUCTION

*Chocolate.*

Otherwise known as my Desert Island (or should that be Dessert Island) item, it's been my favourite food ever since that very first bite. When I was little, I'd get my pocket money each week and whereas all my school friends would save up for months to add to their Sylvanian Families collection, I'd spend mine each Saturday, without fail, on a bar of the good stuff. You see, I come from a long line of chocoholics. My Dad is similarly predisposed, as was his father before him, who for as long as I knew him had a biscuit tin full of all types of chocolatey treats, which was our treasure trove when we used to visit. For birthdays, I used to pore carefully over my Mum's copy of the *Cadbury's Chocolate Cookbook*, meticulously considering each and every cake before selecting my chosen creation for that year's celebration.

Then, when I was twenty-one, I met Mr H. We bonded over our love of all things cacao; I wooed him with my rocky road. It was love at first bite. A few years later, he moved into the flat I was living in and, stuffed into one of his boxes, I spotted a book. His very own copy of THAT chocolate cookbook.

Suffice to say, our children have all inherited the chocoholic gene too. It seemed only right, therefore, to go full circle and create a book that they (and of course you) can enjoy, featuring all my favourite chocolatey recipes, made free from gluten, dairy and refined sugar and using only natural ingredients. This book is for all my fellow chocolate lovers: from snacks to confectionery, cakes to ice cream, crumbles to milkshakes and everything in between, I've got you covered.

If you're familiar with my recipes at all, you'll know that, above all, I always want to make healthier, free-from treats accessible to as many people as possible. This book is no different; everything is simple and easy to make, with minimal ingredients and ones that shouldn't be too hard to seek out either. The recipes in this book are perfect if you're time-poor but you want to snack on something rich and delicious or if you want to create mess, magic and memories with little ones too. I've also tried to include nut-free options wherever I can so that as many people as possible can enjoy these chocolatey delights.

# Chocolate – an ancient love affair

Chocolate is by no means a passing fad; in fact, it can be traced all the way back to the ancient Mayans of Mexico. It is made from cacao beans, which are harvested from cacao pods before being dried and roasted, then ground into a powder. Much like I do, the Mayans revered chocolate, drinking it to toast celebrations and for ceremonial purposes. The Aztecs also used cacao beans as a form of currency – an early version of chocolate coins, if you will! They considered cacao beans to be even more valuable than gold. I can't say I disagree.

Cacao was viewed by these ancient civilisations as sacred, and for good reason. Not only is it full of antioxidants, flavonoids (which can help lower blood pressure) and magnesium, it's also said to have aphrodisiac properties, which might explain how I seem to have had two more children since my first book. Luckily, cacao also contains some caffeine, which might also explain how we manage to keep up with them all.

Once cacao reached Europe in the 1500s, people were going loco for cocoa. They added sugar, milk and spices, and chocolate as we know it was born. Of course, now most store-bought chocolate bars and bakes are mass-produced and contain a lot of ingredients that aren't so natural, but that is exactly where this book comes in. By using raw cacao (instead of cocoa, which is much more processed) in my recipes, the health benefits mentioned above are retained as well.

I'd like to think that the very ancient reverence of all things chocolate has been brought into the twenty-first century through bites of the sweet delights contained in *Vegan Chocolate Treats*. Every recipe has been carefully crafted to ensure that even without gluten, dairy or refined sugar, the most deliciously chocolatey treats are available for everyone to enjoy.

# Cacao deconstructed

When my daughter Azaria was eighteen months old, we took a trip to the Dominican Republic for some glorious winter sun. Whilst running around after a toddler meant I didn't come back with a tan, I did come back with an even greater reverence and understanding of the humble cacao pod. I'd never seen a real one before, and it blew my mind how basically a giant bean can contain not only the cacao beans that are ground up to make cacao powder, but also the cacao butter that is used in chocolate production. So, the cacao pods are basically like a deconstructed chocolate bar – how crazy is that! Just add a little natural sweetener to taste and that's it!

# Chocolate for geeks

If you didn't know it already, I'm a bit of a geek – and sometimes the nerd in me just cannot be suppressed. Luckily, there's some geeky stuff I can tell you about chocolate that will scratch that itch. You see, making it is really like an equation: you need the solid bit that will keep it from being too melty, you need the powder, which will add the flavour and, for most of us (except the hardcore 100% fans), you need something to sweeten it too. And then you can add in other things to flavour it, leave out the cacao powder to make it white chocolate or add in something milky to make it milk chocolate.

Chocolate-making, whilst simple in theory, has developed into nothing short of a fine art. Tempering chocolate requires heating and cooling chocolate to an exact degree, as well as all sorts of complex steps, and it's this process that makes chocolate 'snap'. Luckily, I've simplified things a bit in this book, so no thermometers are needed, unless you want to of course! I'll touch on some of the techniques I've learnt though so that you can try them if you so wish. Another geeky thing about chocolate is that if you melt it and then cool it, it will go back to being solid chocolate again. This is very handy for me (and for you too) as if you make a batch of chocolate, you can store it somewhere and simply melt it or chop it into chunks if any of the recipes call for pre-made chocolate. Of course you can always use shop-bought too, but it's a much cheaper way of having ready-made chocolate that you can add into any recipe where needed.

# Chocolate tips and tricks

Throughout this book I'll share any tips and tricks that I've learnt along the way, but there are a few things I think are useful in many of these recipes. Although I do own a chocolate thermometer, I very rarely use it. I do however always do the following when making chocolate:

* Melt the cacao butter or coconut oil on a low heat. Too hot and it will burn and your chocolate won't be shiny or snap.

* Melt it in a bain-marie (which is not a French woman who likes bathing, but actually a bowl over a saucepan half-full of water), ensuring that the bowl doesn't touch the water.

* Take your bowl out of the saucepan when the solids are around 80% melted and stir to melt the rest. This helps bring down the temperature.

* Wait a little while after you've added your other ingredients before you refrigerate your chocolate or use it for whatever you are making, to allow it to cool and thicken up more for a better consistency.

I also find the following tools really useful for my chocolatey creations:

* Chocolate spiral dipping tools are inexpensive and very easy to use. You can scoop your truffle or ball onto it once you've popped it into melted chocolate, tap it over your bowl to remove any excess and use it to transfer your chocolate-covered item onto a tray without having to touch it and therefore messing up the chocolate before it's solidified.

* Small squeezy sauce bottles are great for getting an even chocolate drizzle or for doing drips around the edges of cakes. Just fill the bottle with melted chocolate and squeeze away!

* Silicone chocolate moulds are great for making chocolates look professional, and for making lovely cake decorations.

* I also have a chocolate-chip mould, which is handy for any recipes that require chocolate chips, as although there are some amazing refined sugar-free chocolate brands out there, it's rare to find refined sugar-free chocolate chips. However, chocolate chunks (just roughly chopped chocolate) work just as well in these recipes, so not to worry if you can't get your hands on one.

# The elements of chocolate

Chocolate, as we know it, requires three main elements: the fat element to make it solid (cacao butter), the chocolatey taste (cacao powder) and a sweetener, as cacao on its own is quite a bitter taste.

## CACAO BUTTER VS COCONUT OIL

Cacao butter is great for making chocolate if you want it to be more solid, for example if you are going to use it as chocolate chunks in a recipe or for covering truffles with, or if you just want to make a chocolate bar or two.

Coconut oil, however, is a much cheaper ingredient to use and great if you want your chocolate to be a little meltier, for example, if you're making fudge.

I find that ordering cacao butter in bulk online (I order it in 1kg bags) makes it a lot more cost-effective. Most coconut oil has a lovely coconutty flavour, but for recipes where I don't want this, I use refined coconut oil, which simply means the coconut meat has been filtered and dried before being pressed into oil.

## THAT CHOCOLATEY TASTE

Many of these recipes contain cacao powder, which I also buy in bulk online. Cacao is similar to cocoa powder, but the latter is roasted at a much higher temperature. This means it loses some of its health benefits, but it can still be used in these recipes if you prefer.

Some of the recipes in this book contain cacao nibs, which I love because they have the cacao flavour but bring a lovely crunchy texture.

## SOMETHING A LITTLE SWEET

To balance out the bitter cacao, I like to add a little bit of natural sweetness into my recipes. I mostly use dates, pure maple syrup and coconut sugar, as well as relying on the natural sweetness of other ingredients such as fruit and oat milk.

I've used Medjool dates throughout this book as they are the softest and juiciest; however they are more expensive than other types of dates. I recommend Deglet Nour as an alternative, and if your dates aren't very soft, soak them in warm water for half an hour, then drain them and they will be soft enough to blend

You'll see coconut sugar being used more in this book than in *Vegan Treats*, as it is now more readily available and fairly cost-effective compared to other unrefined sweeteners.

# Other ingredients

I spoke in detail about the ingredients I like to use in *Vegan Treats*, but I thought it would be good to recap here for anyone new – hi there if that's you!

## NO GLUTEN? NO PROBLEM

I love using ground oats (which is the same as oat flour), ground almonds and buckwheat flour in my recipes instead of wheat flour as they are all gluten-free (check your brand of oats specify gluten-free), natural and unrefined – many flours are bleached or refined, which takes away much of the health benefits they may have. Make your own ground oats by blitzing porridge oats in a clean, dry high-speed blender – it's super quick and so much cheaper than buying oat flour.

## EGG-CELLENT SUBSTITUTES

I use ingredients such as banana, applesauce, flax or chia eggs (which are 1 tablespoon of ground flaxseeds or chia seeds left in 3 tablespoons of water for around 5 minutes as egg replacers). They work well to bind ingredients in the way that eggs do.

## I CAN'T BELIEVE IT'S NOT BUTTER

I find that a combination of nut butter or tahini and coconut oil works well in place of dairy butter. Whilst I know there are products such as margarine or vegan butter out there, I don't love using them due to how processed and refined they can be.

## GOT MILK?

There are so many great milk substitutes out there, my favourites being oat and almond, both of which I like to make from scratch and use in my bakes as well as shop-bought options. I use these milks combined with a little apple cider vinegar to make a buttermilk substitute, which you'll see in some of the recipes in this book.

## NUTS ABOUT COCONUTS

I've got to do a special shout out to the MVP of my style of baking – coconuts. I sound like Bubba Gump but there's coconut oil, coconut sugar, coconut milk, coconut cream, desiccated coconut, the list is endless. They are all amazing when it comes to substitutes for things like sugar, butter, milk and cream.

# Conversions table

I love baking using measuring cups – I find it so much easier than faffing around with scales, but I'm aware that some people do prefer using scales instead. I had so many people tell me how much they loved the conversions table in *Vegan Treats*, so I've popped one in here too for easy reference. I hope you find it useful too!

## LIQUIDS
I find these liquid conversions to be very useful when I'm trying to quickly whip something up in the kitchen and need to measure something like water or plant-based milks

1 teaspoon = 5ml

1 tablespoon = 15ml = ½ fl oz

½ cup = 125ml = 4 fl oz

1 cup = 250ml = 8 fl oz

* NB when making ground oats by blending them, 1 cup of oats will yield around ¾ cup of oat flour.

| Ingredient | ¼ cup | ⅓ cup | ½ cup | 1 cup |
|---|---|---|---|---|
| almonds, whole | 35g | 50g | 70g | 140g |
| almonds, ground | 25g | 33g | 50g | 100g |
| buckwheat flour | 30g | 40g | 60g | 120g |
| cacao butter, solid | 60g | 80g | 115g | 230g |
| cacao nibs | 30g | 40g | 60g | 120g |
| cacao powder | 25g | 35g | 50g | 100g |
| chocolate chunks | 35g | 50g | 70g | 140g |
| cashew nuts, whole | 35g | 45g | 65g | 130g |
| coconut cream | 60g | 80g | 120g | 240g |
| coconut milk | 60ml | 80ml | 125ml | 250ml |
| coconut, desiccated | 25g | 35g | 50g | 100g |
| coconut oil, solid | 50g | 70g | 100g | 200g |
| coconut sugar | 45g | 60g | 85g | 170g |
| dates, Medjool and dried | 40g | 50g | 75g | 150g |
| hazelnuts, whole | 30g | 40g | 60g | 120g |
| maple syrup | 80g | 110g | 160g | 320g |
| nut butters | 60g | 80g | 120g | 240g |
| oats, jumbo/porridge | 25g | 35g | 50g | 100g |
| oats, ground* | 25g | 30g | 45g | 90g |
| peanuts, whole | 40g | 50g | 75g | 145g |
| pecan nuts, halves | 25g | 35g | 50g | 100g |
| pistachio nuts, whole | 40g | 45g | 75g | 125g |
| walnuts, halves | 25g | 35g | 50g | 100g |

This chapter includes many of the delicious chocolatey delights that I make day in and day out, either on their own or as elements within other recipes.

Some of the recipes in this chapter feature heavily in our daily breakfast routine: granola, pancakes, chocolate spread, overnight oats and milkshakes to name but a few. Young me would have thought I'd hit the jackpot being able to start my day with something chocolatey – my kids think the same, but little do they know there's also a whole lot of goodness in there too.

This chapter is also home to some of my all-time favourite things to add that *je ne sais quoi* to make the perfect bake. Think chocolate ganache and dreamy buttercream frosting for celebration cakes, super-smooth chocolate caramel and chocolate sauce for drizzling on top of desserts, and of course a recipe for, well, chocolate itself!

# Chapter 1

\*

# MY SIMPLE CHOCOLATE STAPLES

# VELVETY CHOCOLATE SPREAD

NUT-FREE

When I was little, I used to love going for sleepovers at my grandparents' house. I would watch Saturday morning TV, dress up in my grandma's high heels and jewellery and eat toast with chocolate spread on for breakfast. Once they had run out of chocolate spread, so my grandma actually melted a bar of chocolate for us to have on our toast instead. She was a terrible cook (as my grandpa often liked to point out – he'd even ask the dog if he'd like to swap dinners) but this was definitely one of her better creations.

Anyway, chocolate spread always takes me back to those Saturday mornings, where having fun was pretty much the only rule. So, I've created my own version and it's simply divine. Velvety, smooth and nut-free: tell your toast it's getting an upgrade! * *makes 1 jar*

> 250ml (1 cup) full-fat coconut milk
> 6 Medjool dates, pitted
> 35g (⅓ cup) cacao powder
> pinch of Himalayan salt

1. Place the ingredients in a saucepan and bring to the boil, then simmer on a low heat for 15 minutes.

2. Leave to cool for 5 minutes, then pour this mixture into a high-speed blender and whizz until it forms a smooth, chocolatey mixture.

3. Spoon this into an airtight glass jar and leave to cool before placing the lid on and refrigerating for 2 hours.

4. Store in the jar in the fridge for up to 2 weeks.

# CHOCOLATE BROWNIE HUMMUS DIP

NUT-FREE

I love hummus. I love chocolate. And wouldn't a sweet (and protein-packed) chocolate hummus dip be the perfect thing to smother on juicy dates, dollop into your breakfast bowl, spoon onto strawberries or slather onto banana bread? Well, yes. Yes, it is. This stuff literally tastes like a raw chocolate brownie mixture. It requires just a few ingredients, 5 minutes to make and is a great way to get some extra protein into your day too! An all-round win in my opinion.
* *makes 1 bowl*

> 1 x 400g can of chickpeas, drained
> 4 tablespoons cacao powder
> 4 tablespoons coconut sugar
> 80g (¼ cup) pure maple syrup
> 2 tablespoons tahini
> 1 tablespoon water
> pinch of Himalayan salt

1. Simply blend all the ingredients in a high-speed blender or food processor until the mixture reaches a smooth consistency.

2. Spoon into an airtight container and store in the fridge for up to 3 days.

## Top tip

Save the aquafaba (chickpea water) from the can, and use it to make my honeycomb bars on page 53.

# A CHOCOLATE MILKSHAKE TO BRING ALL THE BOYS TO THE YARD

**NUT-FREE**

When I was younger, we once went on holiday to a hotel that did the most amazing chocolate milkshakes. My brother and I were obsessed, and we'd slurp two or three before lunchtime each day, including once before a rather choppy trip on a boat to go snorkelling, where I slightly regretted having that extra milkshake. Not sure my parents were that impressed when the bill came at the end of our trip either. Looking back, maybe those choppy seas were just karma doing its thing, *Moana*-style. My daughter Azaria is also very partial to a chocolate milkshake, and this one is a favourite of hers too. * *serves 1*

1 frozen sliced banana
360ml (1½ cups) oat milk
1 tablespoon cacao powder
1 teaspoon pure maple syrup

Simply pop the ingredients in a blender and whizz until smooth, then pour into a glass and serve immediately. Enjoy!

## Top tip

To make this even thicker (frappuccino-style), freeze half of the oat milk into ice cubes before blending.

# MY SECRET CHOCOLATEY GRANOLA

NUT-FREE *option*

When lockdowns hit, the cafés I supply desserts to closed and cake orders dried up for a little while as no one was having parties (well, outside of Number 10 Downing Street), so I decided to post out some treats to order. I never imagined how popular they'd be, especially my granola, which was described by many as 'addictive' and even as 'vegan crack'. Every time I shared a photo online, I'd have a flurry of requests for the recipe, which until now I've kept to myself. But it seemed only fair to share it in this book because I've never been able to keep a secret, and this recipe is just too good! * *makes 1 big jar*

3 tablespoons coconut oil
6 tablespoons pure maple syrup
120g (½ cup) peanut butter
   (use a seed butter or tahini to make nut-free)
4 tablespoons cacao powder
pinch of Himalayan salt
300g (3 cups) jumbo oats

*Optional extras*
chopped Medjool dates
cacao nibs
coconut flakes
chocolate chips

1. Preheat your oven to 180°C/gas mark 4.

2. Pop the coconut oil in a saucepan, place on a low heat and stir until totally melted. Add in the maple syrup, peanut butter, cacao powder and salt and stir well, then remove from the heat and stir in the oats. Once this is all mixed together, spoon the granola onto a lined baking tray.

3. Bake for about 15 minutes, then take out of the oven and stir before baking for a further 5 minutes.

4. Once it has cooled, add in any extra ingredients and store in an airtight container at room temperature for up to 3 weeks.

# THE ULTIMATE LUXURY HOT CHOCOLATE

NUT-FREE *option*

Whenever I get to pick up my daughter from school on my own, we take a little detour and sneak off to a café on our walk home for a hot-chocolate date, before we arrive back home to 'those naughty boys' as she calls them. This hot chocolate is one that we make at home when we don't manage to get our little date in, but luckily she likes it just as much. It's thick, creamy, rich and chocolatey, and it takes me right back to getting 20p hot chocolates from the vending machine at school to warm myself up (and get my little chocolate fix). Heaven in every sip – just be sure to let it cool a little before you slurp away! * *serves 2*

480ml (2 cups) oat milk
3 tablespoons cacao powder
2 tablespoons pure maple syrup
4 tablespoons cashew butter
   (or coconut cream to make it nut-free)
pinch of Himalayan salt

1. Pop the ingredients in a blender and blend for about a minute until smooth and chocolatey! Continue blending until hot if you have a high-speed blender or, if not, then heat the mixture in a saucepan on a medium heat, stirring occasionally, until it reaches your desired drinking temperature.

2. Best enjoyed with a dollop of coconut cream and a side of chocolate biscuits for dunking!

# CHOCOLATE PANCAKE STACK

Despite being a Jewish/atheist household, when it comes to Pancake Day, we are all in. Since 2009 we've hosted an annual pancake party, with a few missed years when I was inconveniently giving birth, and these pancakes have stolen the show every year. They now feature as a regular weekend breakfast in the café I seem to be running out of my kitchen. If you're wondering, it's the kind of café where Mum is the Maître d'/ sous-chef/waitress/cleaner and everything in between, all the customers insist on ordering off-menu items and no one ever pays the bill.

These only require seven ingredients for both the pancakes and the sauce, and they are so fluffy with the most heavenly sauce. Add some strawberries on top for the best stack ever! ✳ *makes a stack of 5 pancakes*

*For the pancakes*
125g (1¼ cups) porridge oats
3 ripe bananas
35g (⅓ cup) cacao powder
250ml (1 cup) almond milk
2 tablespoons pure maple syrup
120g (½ cup) cashew butter
2 tablespoons coconut oil, for frying

*For the sauce*
1 tablespoon coconut oil
60ml (¼ cup) almond milk
2 tablespoons cacao powder
2 tablespoons cashew butter
2 tablespoons pure maple syrup

1. For the pancakes, whizz the oats in a blender for about a minute until they become a flour.

2. Add in all the other pancake ingredients except the coconut oil and whizz again until you have a thick batter.

3. For the sauce, melt the coconut oil in a saucepan on a medium heat, then stir in the other ingredients until you have a thick sauce.

4. Pop a tablespoon of coconut oil in a frying pan on a medium heat and, once melted, dollop large spoonfuls of the mixture into the pan. Leave the pancakes to cook for a couple of minutes (2–3 minutes each side is usually enough), then flip over with a spatula to cook the other side too. Continue until you've used all the batter, adding in more coconut oil if you need.

5. Stack up the pancakes on a plate and pour the sauce on top. Serve straight away, adding any berries on top if you fancy.

*Top tip*
Make sure your blender is totally dry before blending the oats to get the smoothest flour possible.

# DREAMY BUTTERCREAMY FROSTING

This frosting is my ultimate favourite.
It glides onto cupcakes and the texture
is just wonderful. You'd never know there's
avocado in it, and for anyone questioning
the method in my madness, it is the said
avocado that gives it a wonderful buttery
consistency. So much so, that when
I've finished making it, there's always a
queue of small people next to me, patiently
waiting for their lick of the spoon.

*makes 1 bowl*

130g (1 cup) cashews, soaked in
   hot water for at least 4 hours
240g (1 cup) coconut cream
6 tablespoons cacao powder
100g (½ cup) coconut oil
160g (½ cup) pure maple syrup
1 ripe avocado

1. Drain the cashews, then place all the ingredients
   in a food processor and blend for around 5 minutes,
   stopping every couple of minutes to scrape down
   any mixture that has climbed up the sides of the bowl.

2. Continue blending until the mixture is smooth and
   creamy, then spoon it into a bowl and place it in the
   fridge for 20 minutes to set.

3. Spoon or pipe the frosting onto cakes
   or cupcakes or freeze it for up to
   2 months to use in the future.
   Once frosted, keep any cakes in the
   fridge and consume within 3 days.

# DOUBLE-CHOCOLATE OVERNIGHT OATS

NUT-FREE

Overnight oats but make them indulgent. This twist on everyone's favourite easy on-the-go breakfast takes them from 0–100 in just a few simple steps! Chocolatey and sweet oats topped with a chocolate shell, which is not only incredibly tasty but also serves as an extra layer of protection if you're taking these to eat on the run and you're worried about potential leakage. Tapping into that chocolatey layer reminds me of being little and tapping into a crème brûlée – but so much better. My little ones love these, they are such a treat but with all the good stuff too! Mix them up by adding in fruit or nut butter. You can switch out the tahini if you don't have any to hand or if you're not into it. Just swap it for equal amounts of any other nut or seed butter. *makes 1 jar*

### For the overnight oats
50g (½ cup) porridge oats
1 tablespoon chia seeds
125ml (½ cup) oat milk
1 teaspoon tahini
1 teaspoon cacao powder
1 teaspoon pure maple syrup

### For the chocolate shell
1 tablespoon coconut oil, melted
1 teaspoon pure maple syrup
1 teaspoon cacao powder
1 teaspoon tahini

1. Mix the oats and chia seeds in a bowl, then add the other overnight oats ingredients and stir until well combined. Pour the mixture into a jam jar or similar.

2. For the shell, combine the ingredients in a bowl and stir well, then pour on top of the oat mixture. Place the lid on and refrigerate overnight (clue is in the name, right?) before serving.

3. Store in the fridge for up to 5 days.

# MY STAPLE CHOCOLATE RECIPE

NUT-FREE

I make this recipe day in, day out, not just for chocolates but for cake decorations, dipping truffles in, drizzling on desserts and also for making chocolate chunks to add into other bakes. You'll see this recipe referenced a lot in this book, so if you've got any sticky tabs, stick one right here. I love doubling up my batch, so I always have some on hand to chop into chunks or to melt down. You can jazz it up too, by adding in some cashew butter to make it more 'milky' or some orange extract or chopped nuts, for example. The possibilities, much like my love for chocolate, are endless! *makes 1 batch*

230g (1 cup) cacao butter
50g (½ cup) cacao powder
4 tablespoons pure maple syrup
pinch of Himalayan salt

1. Place the cacao butter in a bowl, then pop it in a saucepan half-full of water, making sure the bowl is not touching the water. Heat on a low heat until about 80 percent melted, then remove from the heat and stir until the rest dissolves.

2. Add in the other ingredients (you can use more or less maple syrup, according to taste) and continue stirring until you have a smooth, glossy chocolate mixture.

3. Allow the mixture to cool for a few minutes before carefully spooning it into silicone moulds, then refrigerate for around 15 minutes to set. If using for truffles or drizzling on desserts, use straight from the bowl, but if saving to do this for later, I like to let it set in ice-cube moulds so I can easily pop it out and melt gently at a future date. For using as chocolate chunks I would spoon the mixture into bar-shaped moulds or a lined baking loaf tin which can easily be chopped up into chunks.

4. Keep any leftovers in the fridge for up to a week or freeze for up to 2 months.

# CHOCOLATE GANACHE (WHITE AND MILK)

After giving up dairy and refined sugar, I spent many sleepless nights mourning the end of my lifelong love of chocolate ganache. Luckily for me though, it seems that I've found the answer. An answer that means I sleep much more soundly, tucked up and dreaming of rivers of smooth, rich, thick chocolate.

This ganache is incredibly versatile. I use it for frosting cupcakes and filling cakes, but I also love popping it into ice-cube moulds, freezing them and then coating in melted chocolate for the most wonderful truffles.

* *makes enough to cover a cake*

### For milk chocolate
(omit the cacao powder and replace with
½ teaspoon vanilla extract for white chocolate)
65g (½ cup) cashews, soaked in
    hot water for 2 hours
60g (¼ cup) cacao butter, melted
2 tablespoons coconut cream
25g (¼ cup) cacao powder
3 tablespoons pure maple syrup

1.  Drain the cashews then place them and the rest of the ingredients in a high-speed blender. Whizz for a minute or so until you have a smooth mixture, stopping every 20 seconds to scrape any excess down the sides of the blender.

2.  If you're using the ganache for frosting cupcakes, place it in a bowl in the fridge for 10 minutes to firm up. Otherwise spoon it onto your cakes or into your mouth straight up!

3.  Store any leftovers in the fridge for up to 5 days or freeze for up to 2 months.

# CHOCOLATE CARAMEL

**NUT-FREE**

People often tell me I'm a total magpie. Caramels were always one of my favourites in the chocolate box – I could spot their golden wrappers a mile off and was always quick to nab one before it was only the coffee creams left. Yeuch. I'm so excited that I can now make my very own and use it in my creations to my heart's desire. I included a caramel recipe in my first book, but obviously I had to make a chocolate version for this one, and it's so good! Perfect for drizzling over desserts or for chocolate fillings. No shiny wrappers these days, but it still tastes just as delicious.

* *makes 1 small jar*

85g (½ cup) coconut sugar
180ml (¾ cup) plus 2 tablespoons
    full-fat coconut milk
1 tablespoon cacao powder
pinch of Himalayan salt

1.  Add the coconut sugar and coconut milk to a saucepan on a medium to high heat and stir it until the sugar dissolves completely, then bring to a boil and simmer on a low to medium heat for around 30–40 minutes, stirring until it just begins to thicken and has turned a dark amber colour.

2.  Remove the pan from the heat and stir in the cacao powder and salt, then leave to cool completely.

3.  Spoon into an airtight jar or straight onto your dessert!

4.  Store in the fridge for up to 2 weeks.

### Top tip
The caramel will thicken up as it cools, so remove from the heat whilst still runny, otherwise it will be too hard once cool.

# SAUCY CHOCOLATE SAUCE

**NUT-FREE**

At school, my favourite day of the week was Friday, as aside from the obvious impending weekend, the canteen served chocolate sponge with chocolate sauce and it was famously good. The bowls would be laid out on a counter and it was a race to grab the one with the most sauce. Safe to say, my love of both chocolate sauce and of Fridays hasn't diminished since. This one is so easy to make, and perfect on gooey chocolate brownies, bowls of ice cream or for dipping fruit into. * *makes 1 small jar*

2 tablespoons coconut oil
2 tablespoons oat milk
80g (¼ cup) pure maple syrup
25g (¼ cup) cacao powder

In a saucepan, melt the coconut oil on a low heat, then stir in the other ingredients. Leave on a low heat for around 5 minutes until it starts to thicken, then pour onto whatever you like!

One thing I've learnt about myself over the years is that I'm a grazer and that I love chocolate. Also that I can't count, because I guess that's two things. I'm also always on the go; running from drop-offs to cake and café deliveries to pickups and everything in between, so having snacks ready to go each day is crucial.

This chapter brings it all together; it's packed full of snacks a-plenty that are perfect for popping in lunchboxes, taking to work, fuelling up after a workout or bribing small people with (or so I've heard).

It seems that a love of snacking is genetic; my little ones would eat chocolate balls all day long if they could and woe betide me if I turn up to the nursery or school gates empty-handed. They love to help make (read: make them into phallic shapes and eat as much as they can get away with before I notice) a batch with me every weekend which I then freeze for the week ahead. Buddy, however, if left unattended will rifle through said freezer, help himself to whatever snacks we've made, and snaffle them secretly from frozen.

*Chapter 2*

\*

# BARS
# & BALLS

# NO-BAKE CHOCOLATE CHAI OAT BARS

Once the kids are in bed, it's time to get hypocritical. Out come all the things we try to steer them away from during the day: TV, treats and eating on the couch. I love nothing more than curling up on the sofa with a great series to watch and a cup of steaming hot chocolate chai (see tip below). The spices just give it the perfect flavour hit and balance out the earthy cacao and the sweet dates.

These bars mimic my favourite evening tipple. They're sweet, spiced to perfection and the perfect accompaniment to a cup of chai, day or night. Sometimes I'll have one in the afternoon to keep myself going until the little people are all tucked up in bed asleep.
* *makes a 20cm (8in) square tray-full (16 squares)*

300g (2 cups) pitted Medjool dates, soaked in warm water for 10 minutes
100g (1 cup) walnuts
6 tablespoons peanut butter
2 tablespoons coconut oil
100g (1 cup) pecans
200g (2 cups) porridge oats
3–4 tablespoons water

## For the cacao chai spice mix
70g (⅔ cup) cacao powder
1 teaspoon ground cinnamon
½ teaspoon ground ginger
½ teaspoon ground cardamom
½ teaspoon ground cloves
pinch of Himalayan salt

1. Drain the softened dates then place in a food processor with the walnuts, peanut butter, coconut oil and cacao chai spice mix and whizz until they form a sticky mixture, then spoon into a bowl.

2. Place the pecans in the food processor and pulse for around 10 seconds, then add these and the oats into your mixture, mixing them in with your hands to get everything well combined.

3. Add the water, 1 tablespoon at a time, until you can make the mixture into a big ball without it crumbling.

4. Press the mixture into a lined 20cm (8in) square baking tin or mould and freeze for 20 minutes.

5. Cut into bars and store in an airtight container in the fridge or freezer.

## Top tip
You can make the spice mix in advance and store it in an empty spice jar or similar. I like to make extra and add a little coconut sugar and hot oat milk to it for a delicious spiced hot chocolate!

# GRAIN-FREE POWER BARS

I'm always rushing around during the week, doing every unglamorous but necessary errand you can think of, and these bars are my saviour when it comes to snacking.

I wanted to make a grain-free snack bar to mix it up a little, as otherwise by lunchtime I think we could consist of about 90% oats. The best thing about these bars (aside from their taste of course) is that you can make them with anything you have to hand in terms of nuts and seeds, and they're packed with protein and healthy fats to keep you going, whatever you're up to.

I like to make a big batch of these on a Sunday to see me through the craziness of the week. Or at least that's my plan, because often they are all gone by Tuesday after Mr H and the gang get wind of my latest bake. This recipe makes one batch, but maybe double up if you live in a home like mine! ✱ *makes a 20cm (8in) square tray-full (16 squares)*

280g (2 cups) mixed nuts and/or seeds (I like cashews, almonds, Brazils, walnuts, sunflower seeds, pumpkin seeds and linseed)
30g (¼ cup) cacao nibs
80g (½ cup) raisins
35g (¼ cup) ground flaxseeds
25g (¼ cup) desiccated coconut
50g (¼ cup) coconut oil
80g (⅓ cup) almond butter (or sunflower seed butter to make it nut-free (if you're using just mixed seeds)
3 tablespoons pure maple syrup
pinch of Himalayan salt

1. In a food processor, pulse the nuts and seeds for around 10 seconds to break them down a little bit. Pour into a bowl and add in the cacao nibs, raisins, ground flaxseeds and coconut and stir well.

2. In a saucepan, melt the coconut oil on a low heat and stir in the almond butter, maple syrup and salt until well combined, then pour over the other ingredients and stir well.

3. Spoon the mixture into a lined 20cm (8in) square baking tin or mould, then press down evenly and freeze for 3 hours. Cut into slices and store in the fridge or freezer.

## *Top tip*
Instead of buying a bag of each different type of nut and seed, you can buy mixed bags in the supermarket, which can be added straight into this recipe!

# CHOC-CHIP BREAKFAST BARS

I'm definitely a Jewish mother at heart. 'Have you had enough breakfast?' I'm always asking my little ones. Because what if they haven't, or what if they are having a growth spurt, or what if they get to school/nursery and they are suddenly starving? The worrying is endless. But these bars set my mind at ease. Many schools don't allow nuts, and some don't allow chocolate, so I stick to cacao nibs when I'm making this for weekdays (because they are practically beans, right? Don't tell school), but on weekends I go all out and whack in some chocolate chunks instead. Not only are these delicious, but they are full of good energy and fibre and great for packing in a snack bag to ward off any pesky hunger pangs before lunchtime, or beyond! * *makes a 20cm (8in) square tray-full (16 squares)*

200g (2 cups) jumbo oats
50g (½ cup) desiccated coconut
70g (½ cup) mixed seeds
2 tablespoons chia seeds
2 large ripe bananas (yields ¾ cup puréed)
80g (¼ cup) pure maple syrup
1 tablespoon coconut oil
40g (⅓ cup) cacao nibs or chocolate chunks (vegan store-bought or make your own, see page 21)

1. Preheat your oven to 180°C/gas mark 4.

2. Add the oats, coconut, seeds and chia seeds to a bowl and mix well.

3. Blend the bananas in a bowl until there are no lumps, then stir in the maple syrup and coconut oil. Add this to the dry ingredients.

4. Finally, mix in the cacao nibs or chocolate chunks and press the mixture into a lined 20cm (8in) square baking tin or mould.

5. Bake for 25 minutes or until golden on top, then leave to cool completely before slicing.

6. Store in an airtight container for up to a week or freeze for up to 2 months.

# DOUBLE-CHOCOLATE CRANBERRY BROWNOLA BARS

NUT-FREE *option*

Two things you may not know about me: I love wordplay (no pun left behind) and I'm extremely indecisive. The former is I'm sure one of the things that Mr H likes best about me (although he won't admit it) and the latter is one of the things that I'm sure annoys him the most about me. The 'what takeaway shall we have' question regularly becomes a lengthy debate in my head, much to his frustration. These brownola bars however are two of my favourite things in one – brownies and granola – so I don't have to choose. They are so divine and the cranberries give them the most delicious pop of flavour. The only thing I have to decide is how many to have! ✳ *makes a 20cm (8in) square tray-full (16 squares)*

200g (2 cups) porridge oats
50g (½ cup) cacao powder
100g (1 cup) ground almonds (sub with ground oats to make nut-free)
pinch of Himalayan salt
100g (½ cup) coconut oil, melted
45g (¼ cup) coconut sugar
6 tablespoons pure maple syrup
45g (⅓ cup) dried cranberries
70g (½ cup) chocolate chunks (vegan store-bought or make your own, see page 21, optional)

1.  Preheat your oven to 180°C/gas mark 4.

2.  In a bowl, stir your oats, cacao powder, ground almonds and salt together.

3.  In another bowl, mix together the coconut oil, coconut sugar and maple syrup, then pour this into the dry ingredients and stir well. Finally, stir in the cranberries.

4.  Transfer the mixture to a lined 20cm (8in) square baking tin or mould. Bake for 20 minutes and leave to cool.

5.  Melt the chocolate, if using, on a low heat in a bowl over a saucepan half-full of water, making sure the bowl is not touching the water, then drizzle it on top.

6.  Place the tray in the fridge to allow the chocolate to set, then cut into slices and store in an airtight container for up to a week or freeze for up to 2 months.

# MATCHA-CHOCO COCONUT BALLS

These balls are my favourite snack for when I need a little energy boost. I love matcha (powdered green tea) lattes as a coffee alternative because I can't really tolerate caffeinated coffee anymore and matcha seems to have a much gentler caffeine in it that doesn't give me the jitters. As does cacao. Because some days with three crazy kids, I definitely need something to get me through!

These balls are therefore the perfect thing if you need a little lift, not to mention that they are totally delicious. They're also a favourite in the cafés I sell them to.

I love coating them in some matcha and coconut too – it makes them look like little tennis balls! Game, set and matcha.

*makes 12 balls*

*For the matcha balls*
300g (2 cups) Medjool dates
130g (1 cup) cashews
100g (1 cup) desiccated coconut
4 tablespoons cacao powder
½ teaspoon matcha powder

*To decorate*
50g (½ cup) desiccated coconut
½ teaspoon matcha powder

1.  Blend the matcha ball ingredients in a food processor for around 3 minutes, until you can take a small handful of the mixture and easily shape it into a ball. If the mixture is too crumbly, add in some water, a tablespoon at a time, and continue to blend until it becomes sticky enough to shape into balls.

2.  Place the balls on a chopping board. In a bowl, mix the coconut with the matcha powder using a spoon, then roll the balls one by one in the coconut mix.

3.  Store in the fridge for up to a week or freeze for up to 2 months.

## Top tip
If you don't have any matcha to hand, don't worry! These balls are just as tasty without it.

## ITSY-BITSY TAHINI PROTEINY BALLS

**NUT-FREE** *option*

In my first year of senior school, our year seven 'choir' (in the loosest sense of the word) performed the song 'Itsy-bitsy Tahini Proteiny Yellow Polka Dot Bikini'. Or something like that; I never could get the words quite right. Anyway, my obsession with tahini knows no bounds. It's a little-known fact that I eat some savoury food too (in between desserts), and tahini is often a staple in my salad dressings, hummus and drizzled over roasted veggies. But it's also an excellent substitute for nut butter, and I love using it in sweet recipes too. These balls are perfect for a protein hit, whether you're after a post-workout treat, a teatime boost or just a little snack. * *makes 12 balls*

> 225g (1½ cups) Medjool dates
> 70g (½ cup) almonds
>    (sub with oats to make nut-free)
> 120g (½ cup) tahini
> 1 tablespoon unflavoured vegan
>    protein powder (optional)
> 1 tablespoon coconut oil
> 3 tablespoons cacao nibs
> 35g (⅓ cup) cacao powder
> pinch of Himalayan salt

1. Place the ingredients in a food processor and whizz for around a minute until the ingredients form a sticky mixture.

2. Roll this into evenly sized balls and store in the fridge for a week or freeze for up to 2 months in an airtight container.

## CRUNCHY BUCKWHEAT BALLS

These are the balls I go back to making over and over again, every single week. I usually make them on a Sunday afternoon, while the others are chilling out on the sofa with a film on because apparently, when I am at home, I am one of those people who are unable to sit down.

I have one of these balls every night as a proverbial pat on the back once the kids have gone to sleep, and I don't mean to go all Marie Kondo on you (although my wardrobe, and indeed my husband, probably wish I would) but these really do 'spark joy'. The buckwheat, macadamias and cacao nibs make them perfectly crunchy, balanced out by the almost fudgy texture that the other ingredients bring. * *makes 12 balls*

> 300g (2 cups) Medjool dates
> 240g (1 cup) cashew butter
> 4 tablespoons cacao powder
> 2 tablespoons coconut oil
> pinch of Himalayan salt
> 65g (½ cup) macadamias
> 45g (¼ cup) buckwheat groats
> 30g (¼ cup) cacao nibs

1. Place the dates, cashew butter, cacao powder, coconut oil and salt in a food processor and whizz until they form a sticky, chocolatey mixture.

2. Add in the other ingredients and blend for a further 10 seconds, so that the nuts are roughly chopped.

3. Roll into balls and store in the fridge for up to a week or freeze for up to 2 months.

# TRAIL MIX BALLS

Trail mix, also known as 'scroggin' (what a name), is a mix of granola, nuts, dried fruit and sometimes chocolate, designed to be taken on hikes because it's lightweight and a great energy booster. I discovered it when I did a summer school programme at Harvard University, and you could go to the dining hall at 9pm for 'brain food'. Trail mix (with chocolate chips) was always on the menu and I pretty much ate it by the bowl. Not sure about brain food, but it definitely gave me a great energy boost to hike all the way to the club and party until 3am every morning . . . those were the days!
*makes around 14 balls*

65g (½ cup) cashews
225g (1½ cups) Medjool dates
120g (½ cup) peanut butter
100g (1 cup) porridge oats
40g (¼ cup) pumpkin seeds
45g (⅓ cup) dried cranberries
40g (⅓ cup) cacao nibs or chocolate chunks
   (vegan store-bought or make your own, see
   page 21)

1.  Pulse the cashews in a food processor for around 10 seconds, then pop them in a bowl.

2.  Add the dates, peanut butter and half of the oats into the food processor and blend until you have a sticky mixture, then place in a bowl and, with your hands, knead in the other ingredients.

3.  Roll into balls and store in an airtight container in the fridge for up to a week or freeze for up to 2 months.

# PRALINE-FILLED TRUFFLE BALLS

I've loved pralines since a school trip to Belgium, where I spent all my money in the most amazing truffle shop. Mr H and I went on a weekend to Brussels many years ago, on a pretty tight budget, and the pralines in the chocolate shops were so delicious we'd try to work out when the shop assistants changed shift so we could pop back in to get another free sample. The combination of sweet, chocolate and almond is total perfection. These balls not only look delicious, but once you bite into them you're in for the most delicious surprise! *makes 12–14 balls*

*For the filling*
6 tablespoons almond butter
2 tablespoons cacao powder
2 tablespoons pure maple syrup
2 tablespoons coconut cream
pinch of Himalayan salt

*For the balls*
225g (1½ cups) Medjool dates
60g (½ cup) hazelnuts
3 tablespoons almond butter
4 tablespoons cacao powder
2 tablespoons coconut cream

1.  To make the filling, combine the ingredients in a bowl and stir well, then pour it into chocolate moulds or ice cubes (one teaspoon into each section) and freeze for 2 hours or until solid.

2.  Blend the ingredients for the balls until they form a sticky mixture. Make the mixture into around 12 balls, then flatten them into little pancake shapes.

3.  Place a cube of the filling mixture into the middle of each pancake, fold the ball over it and shape back into a ball. Leave for a few minutes to allow the filling to defrost, then bite in and enjoy.

4.  Store in the fridge for up to a week or freeze for up to 2 months.

# 3-INGREDIENT GANACHE BROWNIE CAKE POP BALLS

I try not to waste food, but as a baker there are always bits of cake offcuts or brownie edges knocking around in the kitchen, as well as extra chocolate. Of course, I could eat it all on the rocks (I often do), but I also love making them into something a little special.

I actually made these to prove a point because Mr H says he doesn't like leftovers. If ever I cook dinner and there's some for the next day I'll eat it, but he won't touch it. More fool him, because I'm pretty sure it's universally agreed that food tastes better the day after it's been cooked, am I right? Anyway, I made these with leftover brownies and chocolate and when he appeared, sniffing around them, I said, 'Oh you won't like these, I made them with leftovers.' Turns out he does like some leftovers after all!

✳ *makes around 12 balls*

210g (1½ cups) chocolate chunks (vegan store-bought or make your own, see page 21)
120g (½ cup) coconut cream
½ a 20cm (8in) square tray-full of brownies or any leftover chocolate cake

*To decorate* (optional)
**chopped nuts**
**desiccated coconut**
**freeze-dried strawberry pieces**

1. Put half of the chocolate in a bowl set over a saucepan half-full of water, making sure the bowl is not touching the water, and melt over a low heat, then stir in the coconut cream.

2. Pour into a mixing bowl, crumble the cake or brownies into the bowl, and then stir well.

3. Place the mixture in the fridge for 10 minutes to harden up, then roll into balls, place on a chopping board covered with baking paper and put back in the fridge while you melt the rest of the chocolate.

4. Dip the balls in the melted chocolate one by one and place them back on the paper, sprinkling any decorations on while the chocolate is wet.

5. Store in an airtight container in the fridge for up to a week or freeze for up to 2 months.

I'm not saying it's the *only* reason I chose it, but the senior school I went to had a tuck shop. Each break time a *Lion King*-esque stampede would occur because if you weren't in the queue in time, the shutters would close and you'd be told to tuck off back to class.

This chapter is my own little tuck shop – but with no queue or last orders. I've included my versions of the best chocolate bars and I've also thrown in truffle recipes that will knock your socks off, as well as a Cornish fudge that tastes so true to form that you'll start smelling sea air and hearing seagull noises.

So although, to quote Forrest Gump, 'life is like a box of chocolates', the second part of that quote doesn't hold true when you've got this chapter at your disposal. You'll know exactly what you're going to get, and mark my words it will all be delicious.

*Chapter 3*

\*

# MY LITTLE
# TUCK SHOP

# CHOC-NUT TRUFFLES

Brangelina. Bennifer. Kimye. Sometimes when you put two good-looking things together, you can create a powerhouse. And, like most celebrity relationships, these truffles won't last very long at all. They're a smooth, silky truffle filling covered by a hazelnut chocolate shell. Once you bite in through the delicious crunchy exterior, you won't believe how smooth and melty the centre is. Heaven in every bite and worth celebrity status! * *makes around 30 truffles*

## *For the truffles*
115g (½ cup) cacao butter
4 tablespoons cacao powder
3 tablespoons pure maple syrup
4 tablespoons hazelnut butter
4 tablespoons coconut cream
pinch of Himalayan salt

## *For the dark chocolate coating*
115g (½ cup) cacao butter
4 tablespoons cacao powder
3 tablespoons pure maple syrup
6 tablespoons chopped roasted hazelnuts
pinch of Himalayan salt

1. To make the truffles, melt the cacao butter in a bowl over a saucepan half-full of water on a low heat, making sure the bowl is not touching the water.

2. Pour into a mixing bowl and combine with the other ingredients, stirring until you have a smooth, creamy mixture. Pour this into ice-cube moulds (or cake cases if you don't have moulds) and pop in the freezer for an hour to set.

3. To make the chocolate coating, melt the cacao butter as above, then add in the other ingredients and stir. Remove the truffles from the freezer and dip each one in the chocolate in turn. Once they've all been dipped, you can use any extra chocolate to dip again and make them extra chocolatey! Store in the fridge or freezer.

# RASPBERRY TRUFFLES

Raspberries and chocolate are one of my absolute favourite flavour combinations. It's a fairly recent love affair (don't tell chocolate orange), but now any time I get my hands on a raspberry-filled chocolate, it's gone before Mr H has a chance to ask for a bite. Coincidentally, and as luck would have it, raspberries are the only berries my kids don't seem to like. They'll eat strawberries and blueberries until the cows come home, which living in Zone 2 of London is probably never. So when I buy raspberries to make these truffles with, they don't disappear from the fridge before I've batted an eyelid. Thank you, universe. * *makes around 15 truffles*

**NUT-FREE**

### For the filling
**60g (¼ cup) cacao butter**
**2 tablespoons cacao powder**
**2 tablespoons pure maple syrup**
**½ teaspoon vanilla extract**
**60g (¼ cup) coconut cream**
**15 raspberries**

### For the chocolate coating
**70g (½ cup) chocolate chunks (vegan store-bought or make your own, see page 21)**

1. Melt the cacao butter in a bowl over a saucepan half-full of water on a low heat, making sure the bowl is not touching the water. Once fully melted, stir in the cacao powder, maple syrup, vanilla, and coconut cream, making sure it is all mixed in well.

2. Spoon a little of the truffle mixture into chocolate moulds, then pop a raspberry in each and continue to fill with the mixture so that the raspberries are covered. Place them in the freezer for 2 hours to set.

3. Melt the chocolate as above, then dunk each truffle in the chocolate, scoop out using a fork and gently place on a chopping board to set. Repeat to use up any excess chocolate and to add more layers!

4. Store in the fridge for up to 5 days or freeze for up to 2 months.

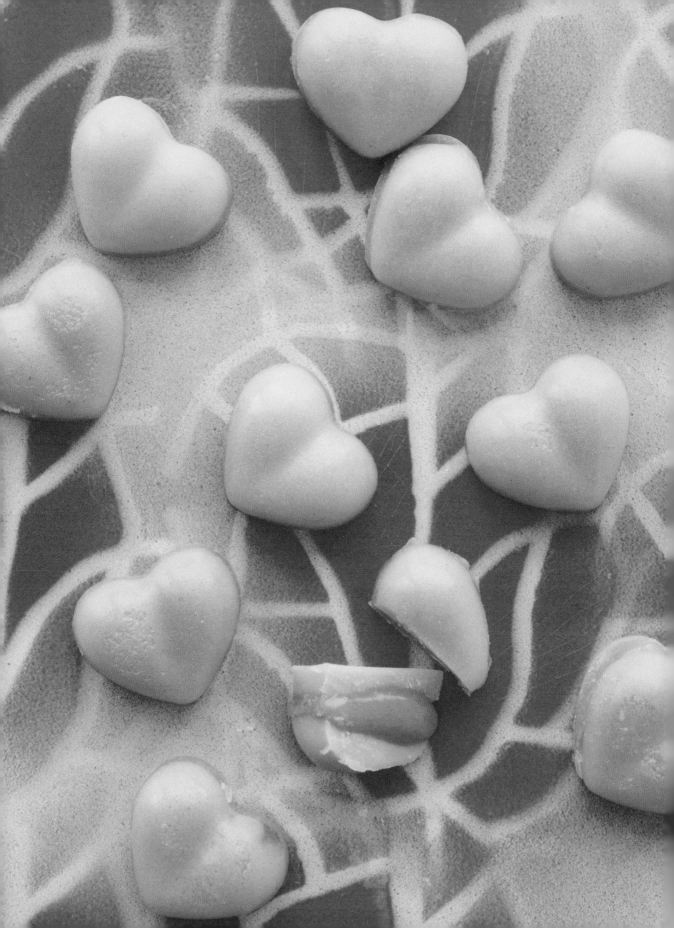

# WHITE CHOCOLATE CARAMELS

Growing up, my brother was always the white chocolate fan in the family, whereas I was more of a milk chocolate kind of girl. He used to frustrate me so much because if anyone were to give us any chocolate, I'd scoff mine right away and he would savour his, eating just a little bit each day.

But now I'm an adult, it's all change: I've become a chocolate savourer too, I've been converted to team white chocolate (well, team all-chocolate, let's be honest) and I'm living with people who would totally scoff all the chocolate, sometimes before I can get a look in, given the chance. I'll let you decide which members of my household I'm referring to there. But let me tell you, these little caramels are pure bites of heaven. I don't think they'd stick around in any household for long!

\* *makes about 14 caramels*

### For the caramels
1 tablespoon almond milk (sub with oat milk to make nut-free)
45g (¼ cup) coconut sugar
1 tablespoon coconut oil
1 tablespoon cashew butter (sub with tahini to make nut-free)
pinch of Himalayan salt

### For the white chocolate
115g (½ cup) cacao butter
2 tablespoons pure maple syrup
2 tablespoons cashew butter (sub with tahini to make nut-free)

1. Place the almond milk and coconut sugar in a saucepan and heat on a medium heat for around 3 minutes (without stirring) until they become a liquid and just begin to bubble.

2. Remove from the heat and stir in the other caramel ingredients until totally combined, then leave it to thicken up and cool while you make the chocolate.

3. To do this, put the cacao butter in a bowl over a saucepan half-full of water, making sure the bowl is not touching the water, and melt over a low heat, then stir in the other ingredients and keep stirring until all combined. Fill your moulds (I use silicone chocolate moulds) one-third full with the white chocolate, then place in the fridge for 10–15 minutes to set.

4. Once set, remove the moulds from the fridge and fill them another one-third full with the caramel mixture.

5. Finally, fill them to the top with the rest of the white chocolate mixture and place in the freezer for 15 minutes to set completely. Remove from the moulds and enjoy!

6. Store in the fridge for up to a week or freeze for up to 2 months.

# LEFT OR RIGHT CARAMEL BARS

Do you remember the advert (in the days when we could only watch actual live TV channels) about whether the left or right finger of a certain two-fingered chocolate bar was better? Well, I sure do, and in my opinion neither one is, because these are. So, two fingers to the shop-bought version because these are so easy to make, and very easy to devour too. Crunchy biscuits topped with gooey caramel and finished with a chocolate coating come together here to make something very special indeed. * *makes 8–10 biscuits*

### For the biscuit base
50g (½ cup) plus 2 tablespoons porridge oats
6 tablespoons ground almonds
pinch of Himalayan salt
60g (¼ cup) cashew butter (or any
　　other nut or seed butter)
80g (¼ cup) pure maple syrup

### For the caramel
60g (¼ cup) cashew butter
2 tablespoons water
40g (¼ cup) Medjool dates, pitted
1 tablespoon coconut oil
pinch of Himalayan salt

### For the chocolate coating
100g (½ cup) coconut oil or cacao butter
3 tablespoons pure maple syrup
4 tablespoons cacao powder
2 tablespoons cashew butter

1. Preheat the oven to 180°C/gas mark 4. To make the base, blitz the oats in a food processor for about 30 seconds until they form a flour then, in a bowl, stir in the ground almonds and salt, followed by the other ingredients, until they form a sticky dough.

2. Split this into 8 to 10 equal-size balls and then either shape them into fingers or pop them in bar-shaped moulds if you have them. Bake in the oven at 180°C/gas mark 4 for 10 minutes. Don't worry if they seem a little soft when they come out as they will harden as they cool.

3. Leave the biscuits to cool for about half an hour, then combine the caramel ingredients in a blender or food processor and whizz for a couple of minutes until smooth.

4. Spoon the caramel on top of the biscuits, using the back of a teaspoon to spread it out evenly, then pop the biscuits in the freezer for around an hour (or longer if you have time; the longer they are there for, the better the chocolate will stick).

5. For the chocolate coating, melt the coconut oil in a bowl over a saucepan half-full of water on a low heat, making sure the bowl is not touching the water, then stir in the other ingredients and mix well.

6. Dunk the biscuits one by one into the chocolate, then repeat until you've used up all the chocolate. Pop them in the fridge for 10 minutes to let them set, then store in an airtight container in the fridge for up to a week.

## Top tips
I like to double up when making the caramel layer and freeze the leftovers. This saves me time when I make these again and they freeze really well.

I use cacao butter in the summer months rather than coconut oil as it can be quite melty in the warmer months.

# THE REAL DEAL CORNISH CHOCOLATE FUDGE

**NUT-FREE**

Fudge for me is so nostalgic; it takes me back to seaside holidays, jelly shoes and rain macs, eating ice cream hiding under umbrellas and the inevitable 'lucky' seagull poo roulette. It always happened to someone, usually my Dad. Fudge was a holiday must too. I used to love the Cornish sweet shops we'd go to where they made every flavour of fudge possible and weighed out your flavours of choice into a brown paper bag. This fudge recipe is inspired by the traditional way of making fudge, but with the ingredients tweaked a little. The nostalgia still hits the same though! ✳ *makes around 8 fudge bites*

2 tablespoons cacao butter
170g (1 cup) coconut sugar
3 tablespoons cacao powder
1 tablespoon plus 1 teaspoon oat milk
pinch of Himalayan salt

1. Place the ingredients in a saucepan and heat on a low to medium heat, stirring until the cacao butter and coconut sugar have dissolved.

2. Remove from the heat and spoon onto a lined tray or mould, then place in the fridge for 2 hours to set.

3. Cut into squares and store in an airtight container in the fridge for up to a week or freeze for up to 2 months.

## Top tips

To mix it up a little, why not stir in some chopped nuts or dried fruit before you place the mixture in the fridge!

# MAS BUENO BAR

'Bueno' in Spanish means 'good', but these bars would be doing themselves a disservice if they just referred to themselves as 'good'. We all need to be our own hype person, right? So, these bars are '*mas bueno*' – or 'better' – because that's exactly what they are. And that's where my Spanish knowledge ends. ✳ *makes 3–4 bars*

*For the hazelnut cream filling*
3 tablespoons hazelnut butter
3 tablespoons coconut cream
1 tablespoon pure maple syrup
pinch of Himalayan salt
10g (⅓ cup) puffed rice

1 batch of my chocolate recipe (see page 21)

1. Mix the first four filling ingredients together in a bowl, then blend the puffed rice until it becomes a coarse flour.

2. Fill small cube moulds (or a small ice cube tray) one-quarter full with the blended puffed rice, then spoon the hazelnut cream onto the top and top with another layer of the puffed rice. Freeze the moulds for 2 hours.

3. Once frozen, take the cubes out of the moulds and line them up in threes on a chopping board or plate covered with baking paper. Place them back in the freezer while you make the chocolate as per the instructions on page 21.

4. Once your chocolate is made, dip each cube into the melted mixture and place them back in their lines of three before the chocolate sets so that the cubes are stuck together in threes to form bars.

5. Store in the fridge in an airtight container for up to a week or freeze for up to 2 months.

# ALMOND NOUGAT BAR

When I was younger, we always used to buy my Dad the biggest Swiss chocolate nougat bar we could find for his birthday. That or socks. When I asked him for ideas of what recipes I could include in this book, his first answer was, 'an almond nougat bar'. I gave some to my Dad to try and, let's just say, I know what to make him for his birthdays now! * *makes 6–8 bars*

*For the almond nougat*
85g (½ cup) coconut sugar
100g (⅔ cup) almonds, chopped into small chunks
pinch of Himalayan salt

*For the chocolate*
230g (1 cup) cacao butter
5 tablespoons cacao powder
5 tablespoons pure maple syrup
pinch of Himalayan salt

1. Place the coconut sugar in a frying pan over a medium heat, stirring occasionally for 5 minutes or until it is melted and amber in colour. It will be sticky and not runny and will burn easily if heated too high.

2. Stir in the chopped almonds and salt and remove the pan from the heat. Place some baking paper on a chopping board and spread the almond sugar mixture onto the paper, then leave it to cool completely. Once cooled, chop into small chunks.

3. Melt the cacao butter in a bowl over a saucepan half-full of water on a low heat, making sure the bowl is not touching the water. Remove from the heat and stir in the other chocolate ingredients.

4. Stir the almond nougat into the chocolate and then spoon this mixture into bar-shaped moulds or cake cases. Place in the fridge for half an hour to set.

5. Store in the fridge for up to a week or the freezer for up to 2 months.

## Top tips

If you really want them to look the real deal, make them in bar moulds then, once set, slice them into chunks and again diagonally into triangles. You can even use a little melted chocolate to stick them together into a bar of triangles!

# CHOCOLATE-COVERED MALT BALLS

NUT-FREE

I've always loved going to the cinema – getting totally lost in a different world and watching stories unfold before my eyes. Plus, when I was little we'd get one of those big boxes of chocolate-covered malt balls to nibble on, and more often than not it would be finished before we'd made it through the trailers. Trailers last for ages though, right? Then, when I met Mr H it turned out that he also loved watching films, and also had a thing for chocolate-covered malt balls. We don't get to the cinema very much these days, but a film on the sofa and a batch of these are just the ticket.

\* *makes 10–15 balls*

### *For the balls*
60g (¼ cup) cacao butter
25g (1 cup) puffed rice
3 tablespoons cashew butter
1 tablespoon coconut sugar
1 teaspoon maca powder
½ teaspoon vanilla extract
pinch of Himalayan salt

### *For the chocolate coating*
¼ batch of my chocolate recipe (see page 21)

1.  Melt the cacao butter in a bowl over a saucepan half-full of water on a low heat, making sure the bowl is not touching the water and stirring gently. Place the puffed rice in a blender or food processor and whizz for around 30 seconds until it has broken down a little (but not completely).

2.  Add in the cashew butter, coconut sugar, maca, vanilla extract and salt and stir, then stir in the crushed puffed rice. Shape them into small balls (mine are a little larger than the traditional Malteser balls) and place in the freezer for 2 hours to set.

3.  Make the chocolate as per the instructions on page 21 then dunk each ball in the melted chocolate one by one, repeating to use up any remaining chocolate. Allow the chocolate to set and dig in!

4.  Store in the fridge for up to a week or freeze for up to 2 months.

# HONEYCOMB BARS

**NUT-FREE**

Honeycomb bars were always right up there in my top chocolate bars. I loved the texture of the honeycomb in the middle, all crunchy but melty too and covered with chocolate – it was just perfection. Creating a healthier version is something I've always wanted to do, but writing this book was the catalyst for finally getting round to it. It took a lot of testing, but I discovered that aquafaba (the liquid from a can of chickpeas) is amazing for making the most delicious vegan honeycomb. I could hardly believe it: chickpea water! You'll be blown away too when you give these a try, I promise!

* makes 8–10 bars depending on size of your baking tray

> 4 teaspoons cornflour
> 160ml (⅔ cup) aquafaba (chickpea water from a can of chickpeas)
> 215g (1¼ cups) coconut sugar
> ½ teaspoon maca powder
> ½ batch of my chocolate recipe on page 21

1. Preheat your oven to 120°C/gas mark ½.

2. Mix the cornflour and aquafaba in a stand mixer on high for around 15 minutes, or until you can see stiff peaks. Add in the coconut sugar and maca powder and mix on high until it has just combined. Pour your mixture onto a baking tray lined with baking paper.

3. Bake for 2 hours, then turn the oven off and leave to cool completely in the oven. Break the cooled mixture into small pieces, then place them in a lined baking loaf tin.

4. Make your chocolate as per the instructions on page 21, then pour it evenly over the malted mixture.

5. Place in the fridge to set, then break or cut into bars. Store in an airtight container in the fridge for up to a week.

# FRUIT AND NUT BARS

I used to adore fruit and nut bars when I was younger. I just loved the texture, the surprise in every bite, not knowing whether the square you'd just snapped off would have a juicy raisin, a crunchy almond or just pure delicious chocolate in it. I'd buy a bar on the weekend with my pocket money and it would be gone by the time I got home from the corner shop. Story of my life. I use cashew butter in this recipe to make them beautifully milky and it works a treat!

* makes about 5 small bars

> 115g (½ cup) cacao butter
> 2 tablespoons pure maple syrup
> 3 tablespoons cacao powder
> pinch of Himalayan salt
> 1 tablespoon plus 1 teaspoon cashew butter
> 2 tablespoons raisins
> 2 tablespoons almonds, roughly chopped

1. Melt the cacao butter in a bowl over a saucepan half-full of water on a low heat, making sure the bowl is not touching the water. Remove once it is mostly melted and stir until completely liquid.

2. Add in the maple syrup, cacao powder, salt and cashew butter and stir until well combined.

3. Finally, stir in the raisins and almonds, then spoon into bar-shaped moulds (or into a lined baking loaf tin and cut into bars once set).

4. Place in the fridge for an hour to set, then store in an airtight container in the fridge for up to a week or in the freezer for up to 2 months.

# CHOCOLATE-COVERED DATES THREE WAYS

I'm a self-confessed Medjool date addict – they are a little more expensive than other types of dates, but they are so juicy, so sweet and just the perfect snack. When we bought our house, we did a lot of the work ourselves and I didn't have time to bake anything, so I'd buy Medjool dates and stuff them with chocolate and nut butter for the best post-DIY treat.

I've since taken them to the next level a little bit, and these are my three favourite combinations. They are unbelievably easy, but with just a few ingredients you can transform your dates into your very own chocolate box! * *makes 1 style per recipe*

8 Medjool dates, pitted

### Hazelnut-chocolate-style

105g (¾ cup) chocolate chunks (vegan store-bought or make your own, see page 21)
1 tablespoon coconut cream
2 tablespoons chopped roasted hazelnuts, plus more to decorate

1. Melt a third of the chocolate in a bowl over a saucepan half-full of water on a low heat, making sure the bowl is not touching the water.

2. Remove from the heat, stir in the coconut cream and the hazelnuts and spoon it into the dates.

3. For the chocolate coating, melt the remaining chocolate chunks as above and dunk the dates in one by one. Sprinkle with chopped hazelnuts.

### Peanut-chocolate-style

1 tablespoon peanuts, roughly chopped
pinch of Himalayan salt
3 tablespoons peanut butter
2 tablespoons cacao nibs

Stir the peanuts and salt into the peanut butter in a bowl. Spoon the mixture into the dates and sprinkle with cacao nibs.

### Coconut-chocolate-style

25g (¼ cup) desiccated coconut
2 tablespoons coconut cream
1 teaspoon pure maple syrup
35g (¼ cup) chocolate chunks (vegan store-bought or make your own, see page 21)

1. Combine the first three ingredients in a bowl and spoon the mixture into the dates.

2. Melt the chocolate in a bowl over a saucepan half-full of water on a low heat, making sure the bowl is not touching the water. Drizzle over the dates.

# WALNUT CONES

When I was younger, my Dad would take my brother and me to the sweet shop on a Saturday morning to spend our pocket money. He'd buy a walnut cone for him and my Mum. I just didn't get it: why would you possibly want to buy something with a nut in when you could just have chocolate? But now I understand. There's something about nuts (and walnuts in particular) that work so well with chocolate, and with the creamy filling they are just straight up delicious. My version is an homage to our little weekend tradition, but without even needing to leave the house. A little biscuit base with a creamy filling all covered in chocolate and topped off with a walnut. * *makes 8 cones*

*For the filling*

65g (½ cup) cashews, soaked in hot water for 2 hours
120g (½ cup) coconut cream
2 tablespoons coconut oil
2 tablespoons pure maple syrup
1 teaspoon vanilla extract

*For the bases*

60g (¼ cup) cashew butter
2 tablespoons pure maple syrup
pinch of Himalayan salt
45g (½ cup) ground oats

½ batch of my chocolate recipe (see page 21), made and left to cool so it begins to thicken up
8 walnuts, for the topping

1.  Drain the cashews and blend with the other filling ingredients in a high-speed blender until they form a smooth, creamy liquid. Place this in a bowl and refrigerate for at least 4 hours to set (or freeze to set quicker). It should be firm to the touch once set.

2.  Whisk the cashew butter, maple syrup and salt for the bases, then once smooth, stir in the ground oats until you have a slightly sticky dough. Roll it out on a piece of floured baking paper and cut out small circles of around 5cm (2in) in diameter. Bake at 170°C/gas mark 3 for 10 minutes, then leave to cool.

3.  Pipe the filling onto the bases by spooning it into a piping bag and piping two circles onto the bases.

4.  Make the chocolate as per the recipe on page 21, making sure it is adequately cooled so that it doesn't melt the filling. Spoon a little of the chocolate into the centre of the circles you have piped, then continue piping smaller circles on top to seal the chocolate in and make a cone shape with the filling.

5.  Place the cones in the freezer for 10 minutes to chill, then quickly dip each upside down into the remaining melted chocolate mixture. Once the chocolate has set, repeat the process for a thicker chocolate coating, then top with a walnut.

*Top tip*

Make sure the chocolate isn't too hot when you're dunking the cones in, so as to not melt the creamy filling.

# SALTED PECAN CARAMEL CUPS

I am, as a Brit, a real Americanophile, which Google tells me is a real word. Because of my numerous trips across the pond, I've discovered many foodie delights, including two of my favourite treats: peanut butter cups and pecan pie. One day, after a moment of daydreaming about these two delights, I decided to put them together and fuse them into one 'megatreat'. * *makes around 10 large (fairy-cake-case-sized) cups*

*For the pecan caramel*
75g (½ cup) Medjool dates, pitted
80ml (⅓ cup) almond milk
50g (½ cup) pecans
4 tablespoons nut butter (I like cashew or almond)
pinch of Himalayan salt

*For the chocolate*
200g (1 cup) coconut oil,
    or 230g (1 cup) cacao butter
6 tablespoons pure maple syrup
8 tablespoons cacao powder
pinch of Himalayan salt

1. Soak the dates in the almond milk to soften them while you make the chocolate. Melt half of the coconut oil or cacao butter in a bowl over a saucepan half-full of water on a medium heat, stirring until it has all melted.

2. Stir in half of the other chocolate ingredients until smooth, then use the chocolate to fill fairy -cake cases (put these on a chopping board or plate first so you can pop them in the fridge easily). Place them in the fridge to set for 15 minutes while you make the caramel.

3. For the pecan caramel, blitz the ingredients, including the soaking milk, in a blender for around a minute until smooth, then when the chocolate base layer is set, spoon about a teaspoon of the caramel into the middle of each cup.

4. Make the remaining chocolate and spoon it on to of each cup, then place them back in the fridge for another 15 minutes until set.

5. Store in the fridge for a week or freeze for up to 2 months.

# RAINBOW 'BRIGADEIROS'

NUT-
FREE

Back when we were footloose and fancy-free, Mr H and I went on a Brazilian adventure. We drank coconuts on Copacabana Beach, danced the night away in Lapa, trekked to hidden beaches on Ilha Grande and marvelled at the sheer beauty of Iguazu Falls. Oh, and we ate. We went to 'kilo' restaurants where you pay for the weight of your plate (our meals came out at vastly different prices) and we discovered brigadeiros – divine little chocolate truffles made with condensed milk and covered in sprinkles. I came home and had to create my own version, with my healthier sprinkles too! ✳ *makes 10–15 small truffles*

1 x 400ml can of full-fat coconut milk
60g (⅓ cup) coconut sugar
2 tablespoons cacao powder

*For the rainbow 'sprinkles'*
100g (1 cup) desiccated coconut

*Natural powders*
matcha (green)
beetroot or pink pitaya powder (pink)
butterfly pea powder (blue)
turmeric (yellow)

1. Put the coconut milk and coconut sugar in a saucepan with a heavy bottom (to avoid burning), stir well and bring to the boil, then reduce to a low heat and simmer for around 45 minutes, stirring every 5 minutes or so. The mixture should be reduced by around half and should have thickened up significantly. When a spoon is dipped in, a thin layer should be left on the spoon when it is lifted out.

2. Add the cacao powder and stir in gently until just mixed in. Do not overmix as this can cause the mixture to separate. Spoon the mixture into a bowl and chill in the fridge for around 90 minutes; it will thicken as it cools.

3. Remove from the fridge and shape into small balls with your hands.

4. Make the rainbow 'sprinkles' by adding desiccated coconut and a little of one of the powders to a bowl and stirring together to colour the coconut.

5. Roll the chocolate balls in the sprinkles.

6. Store for up to 5 days in the fridge or freeze for up to 2 months.

*Top tip*
I like to make a few different bowls of 'sprinkles' and keep any leftovers for cakes or other balls. They look really nice mixed together!

This chapter is proof that opposites attract. Think about it, in every pie, tart or cheesecake you've got the crumbly, firm or biscuity base, living its best life alongside a gooey, creamy or smooth filling. Just how Mr H is tidy where I am messy, laid-back where I am anxious, and humble where I am the funniest person he knows, the flavours and textures in these desserts complement each other and balance out in the tastiest of ways. If these recipes took a relationship test from a '90s teen magazine, they'd score 100% every time.

Whatever you're into, there's something here for you. We're talking fruity flavours like strawberry, banana, passion-fruit, coconut and orange, spicy surprises such as ginger and chilli, as well as all the textures your heart could desire: melt-in-your-mouth truffle pie, crunchy granola, oozing caramel and many more.

*Chapter 4*

\*

# PIES, TARTS & CHEESECAKES

# POPPED RICE STRAWBERRY MOUSSE PIE

NUT-FREE

If you were around in the '90s, you will have had chocolate rice crispy cakes. This delightful dessert has levelled up pie crust by using a chocolatey puffed rice mixture to create the base. The strawberry mousse filling tastes so light and fluffy thanks to its secret (and very clever) ingredient – aquafaba, the artist formally known as chickpea water. * *makes a 20cm (8in) pie*

### For the crust
50g (¼ cup) coconut oil
5 tablespoons pure maple syrup
3 tablespoons cacao powder
50g (2 cups) puffed rice

### For the filling
60ml (¼ cup) aquafaba (chickpea water from a can of chickpeas)
1 teaspoon lemon juice
125g (1 cup) chopped strawberries
2 tablespoons pure maple syrup
120g (½ cup) coconut cream

1. Melt the coconut oil in a saucepan on a low heat, then pour into a bowl and add in the maple syrup and cacao powder and stir well. Fold in the puffed rice, then transfer this to a 20cm (8in) pie dish, pressing it down evenly on the base and sides. Place in the fridge for 2 hours to set.

2. To make the mousse, whip the aquafaba and lemon juice with a stand or hand mixer for around 10 minutes until it starts to get fluffy.

3. In a blender, combine all the other filling ingredients then, once mixed, pour them in with the aquafaba and gently whip them to combine.

4. Pour this filling on top of the base and leave in the fridge for no longer than an hour to set. If it's made too far in advance, it can make the base soggy.

# CHOCOLATE TRUFFLE PIE

We all have those friends. You go to their house for a meal and they pull out all the stops – with a spread fit for royalty. You go home talking about how amazing the food was and then you have a terrible thought. You're going to have to invite them to your house in return, and what if they expect a similarly lavish feast? I've been in that very predicament, and this is what saved my vegan bacon. * *makes a 20cm (8in) pie*

### For the pie crust
125g (1¼ cups) ground almonds
150g (1 cup) Medjool dates
5 tablespoons cacao powder
2 tablespoons coconut oil
pinch of Himalayan salt
1-2 tablespoons water, more if needed

### For the truffle filling
210g (1½ cups) chocolate chunks (vegan store-bought or make your own, see page 21)
180g (¾ cup) coconut cream
120g (½ cup) cashew butter
pinch of Himalayan salt

1. Blend the crust ingredients (except the water) in a food processor, then add water, a tablespoon at a time, until the mixture is slightly sticky and not crumbly. Transfer to a 20cm (8in) pie dish and press the crust mixture down evenly on the base and sides of the tin.

2. Melt the chocolate in a bowl over a saucepan half-full of water on a low heat, making sure the bowl is not touching the water, then remove from the heat and stir in the other filling ingredients. Pour into the base, then set in the fridge for 2 hours, cut into slices and enjoy!

3. Store in the fridge for up to a week or freeze for up to 2 months.

# TRIPLE-CHOC GRANOLA PIE

One benefit of having small children is that I get woken up so often, that I seem to remember a lot more of my dreams. Jokes aside, this pie did actually come to me in a dream, which is funny because when I first made it, I wondered if I was dreaming – it was that tasty. Anyone who knows me will know how much I adore granola (it's a lot) and it makes such a perfect crunchy pie crust. Paired with a silky chocolate filling and crunchy cacao nibs stirred through, this pie is definitely dreamworthy.
* *makes a 20cm (8in) pie*

## Top tip

The base is crunchy and crumbly as good granola should be, but leave it overnight in the fridge to allow it to bind together a little more.

*For the crust*
4 tablespoons coconut oil, plus extra for greasing
130g (1 cup) mixed nuts
240g (1 cup) peanut butter
60g (⅓ cup) coconut sugar
pinch of Himalayan salt
25g (¼ cup) cacao powder
105g (¾ cup) mixed seeds
100g (1 cup) porridge oats

*For the filling*
2 ripe medium avocados
160g (½ cup) pure maple syrup
4 tablespoons peanut butter
50g (½ cup) cacao powder

2 tablespoons cacao nibs, to decorate

1.  Preheat your oven to 180°C/gas mark 4 and melt the coconut oil in a saucepan on a low heat.

2.  Place the nuts in a blender and blend for 20 seconds to break them down a little. Stir the peanut butter, coconut sugar, salt and cacao powder into the coconut oil and remove from the heat, before stirring in the other ingredients.

3.  Spoon this into a greased 20cm (8in) pie dish and use the back of a spoon to press it down evenly on the base and sides. Bake for 15 minutes and leave to cool while you make the filling.

4.  Halve and pit the avocados, scoop the flesh into a blender with the maple syrup, peanut butter and cacao powder and blend for around a minute or until smooth.

5.  Spoon this evenly onto the base and decorate with a sprinkling of cacao nibs.

6.  Place in the fridge for 2 hours to allow the pie to firm up. Store in the fridge for up to 3 days.

# CARAMELISED BANANA, PECAN AND CHOCOLATE GALETTE

NUT-FREE *option*

Don't let the fancy name of this dessert fool you. It's basically a cross between a pancake and a pizza. It's meant to look rustic and it's such an easy and delicious way to impress your friends. You could even say it's easier than pie!

I really love making this with my little ones as it's loads of fun for them to help roll out the dough and pop in the filling. We have had an issue though with the sliced bananas and chocolate chunks disappearing somewhere between measuring them out and actually getting onto the galette. I've got a hunch as to what's been going on, but I know now to always overbudget on the quantities when I'm getting my ingredients out! ✳ *makes a 23cm (9in) galette (serves around 6)*

60g (½ cup) buckwheat flour
45g (½ cup) ground oats
2 tablespoons cacao powder
5 tablespoons coconut oil (not melted)
3 tablespoons oat milk, more if needed
2 tablespoons pure maple syrup

*For the filling*
2 medium bananas, sliced
35g (⅓ cup) pecans, roughly chopped
   (omit to make nut-free)
70g (½ cup) chocolate chunks (vegan
   store-bought or make your own, see page 21)

*For the glaze*
2 tablespoons coconut oil, melted
1 tablespoon pure maple syrup

1. Put the buckwheat flour, ground oats and cacao powder in a bowl and mix well, before adding in the coconut oil and creaming it into the mixture with the back of a spoon.

2. Stir in the oat milk and maple syrup, and then get your hands in and knead it into a dough. If it's at all crumbly, add in a little extra oat milk, 1 teaspoon at a time.

3. Mould the dough into a pancake shape, wrap it in cling film and refrigerate it for 20 minutes.

4. Preheat your oven to 180°C/gas mark 4.

5. Once the dough is chilled, place on a piece of baking paper and roll it out with a rolling pin until it is a rough circle around 23cm wide. Pop it on a baking tray and add the filling ingredients, leaving around 5cm (2in) around the edges.

6. Fold the edges into the middle to create a crust. For the glaze, mix the melted coconut oil and maple syrup in a bowl and using a brush, or dipping kitchen roll into the glaze, brush it onto the crust.

7. Bake in the oven for around 40 minutes. Leave to cool for 10 minutes, then cut into slices and serve, with a dollop of ice cream if that floats your boat!

# SPICED-BISCUIT WHITE CHOCOLATE TART

I used to be an avid follower of fashion, but the trends I follow at the moment seem to be mainly food-related. Sometimes the hype is exactly that, but other times there's a reason behind the obsessions of the masses. In recent years, the emergence of TikTok (which I am definitely too old to understand) seems to have brought with it a load of funny and wacky foodie trends, and I'm 100% here for it. Spiced biscuits seem to have passed absolutely no one by and I am absolutely on the bandwagon. I love the flavour but believe me when I say that combining them with white chocolate elevates things to a whole new dimension. I don't think this tart could ever go out of style!

＊ *makes a 20cm (8in) tart*

*For the spice mix*
¼ teaspoon ground ginger
¼ teaspoon ground mixed spice
2 teaspoons ground cinnamon
¼ teaspoon ground nutmeg
¼ teaspoon ground cloves

*For the biscuit base*
90g (1 cup) ground oats
120g (1 cup) buckwheat flour
130g (¾ cup) coconut sugar
pinch of Himalayan salt
100g (½ cup) coconut oil, melted, plus
    extra for greasing
120g (½ cup) cashew butter
1 teaspoon vanilla extract

*For the white chocolate filling*
60g (¼ cup) cacao butter
3 tablespoons pure maple syrup
80g (⅓ cup) coconut cream
80g (⅓ cup) cashew butter
1 teaspoon vanilla extract

1. Preheat your oven to 180°C/gas mark 4.

2. Make the spice mix in a bowl. Add the ground oats, buckwheat flour, coconut sugar and salt to a bowl and stir. In another bowl, stir together the coconut oil, cashew butter and vanilla until smooth, then pour this into the dry ingredients and knead into a dough.

3. Grease a 20cm (8in) tart tin and press the mixture in evenly, leaving enough aside to make one cookie.

4. Bake the tart and cookie for 15 minutes, until golden. Leave to cool completely.

5. To make the filling, melt the cacao butter in a bowl over a saucepan half-full of water on a low heat, making sure the bowl is not touching the water, then stir in the other ingredients.

6. Pour the filling into the tart tin, then refrigerate for half an hour before serving. Crush the cookie into crumbs and sprinkle on top to serve.

# NO-BAKE CHOCOLATE CARAMEL GANACHE TARTLETS

The way I feel about these tarts is like the way I feel about my children. I adore the sweet chewy chocolate base, then there's the gooey caramel that naughtily oozes out once you bite on it and thirdly there's the gorgeous chocolate ganache on top. I love all the layers equally, but all in such different ways. I simply couldn't pick a favourite, so I need to have all three, please.

These tarts are so decadent and so tasty that they deserve to be on a TV advert, with someone slicing into them in slow motion while 'Albatross' by Fleetwood Mac plays. They are not just any tartlets...

\* *makes around 6 tartlets*

½ batch of my chocolate caramel (see page 22)

*For the base*
150g (1½ cups) porridge oats
4 tablespoons pure maple syrup
4 tablespoons peanut butter (sub with
    tahini to make nut-free)
pinch of Himalayan salt

*For the ganache*
70g (½ cup) chocolate chunks (vegan
    store-bought or make your own, see page 21)
4 tablespoons coconut cream

1. Make the caramel as per the instructions on page 22, then leave to cool while you make the base.

2. Blend the oats in a blender for around a minute until they form a flour, then place in a bowl with the other ingredients for the base and knead with your hands to form a dough. Split this into six then, using cupcake moulds or a lined muffin tin, shape them into mini tarts.

3. Spoon the chocolate caramel equally into the tartlets, then place in the fridge to chill.

4. Melt the chocolate chunks in a bowl over a saucepan half-full of water on a low heat, making sure the bowl is not touching the water, then remove the bowl from the heat and stir in the coconut cream. Spoon this mixture on top of the caramel, then refrigerate for around half an hour before eating.

5. Store in an airtight container in the fridge for a week or in the freezer for up to 2 months.

# CHOCOLATE CUSTARD TARTLETS

If you grew up in the '90s like me, then you'll be no stranger to custard. Dinner ladies in my school canteen would dollop it on anything they could get their hands on – they even made a chocolate version, which was a very popular dish indeed. In our past life (when city breaks and travelling with only hand luggage were a thing for us), Mr H and I went on a wonderful trip to Lisbon, which mainly consisted of sampling sangria and custard tarts, with a bit of sightseeing thrown in for good measure. It seemed only right, therefore, to mix my two most vivid (and delicious) custard memories together, and the result is these scrumptious tarts!

* *makes around 6 tartlets*

*For the pastry*
100g (1 cup) porridge oats
100g (1 cup) ground almonds
5 tablespoons coconut oil, plus extra for greasing
3 tablespoons pure maple syrup
2 tablespoons cacao powder

*For the chocolate custard filling*
130g (1 cup) cashews, soaked in hot water
   for 4 hours
3 tablespoons pure maple syrup
2 tablespoons cacao powder
2 tablespoons coconut oil
½ teaspoon vanilla extract

1.  Preheat your oven to 180°C/gas mark 4.

2.  Place the oats in a food processor and blend for around a minute until they form a flour, then add in the other ingredients and blend again until they form a sticky, smooth mixture.

3.  Press the mixture evenly into greased tartlet tins (you can also use cupcake moulds or a lined muffin tin if you don't have individual tins), then bake for 10 minutes and allow to cool completely.

4.  Drain the cashews then combine the custard ingredients in a food processor or high-speed blender and whizz for around 5 minutes or until smooth.

5.  Spoon into the tartlets and serve immediately.

6.  Store in the fridge for up to 3 days or freeze for up to 2 months.

# CHOCOLATE, PASSION FRUIT AND GINGER CHEESECAKE

Passion fruit was a thing of luxury to me when I was younger. I could never understand why we'd only eat it rarely at home, but whenever I got the chance, I'd always have it – it just tasted so exotic. Now that I'm the person who has to do the fruit cutting, I understand why we never had it at home (it's such a faff to cut for such a small amount of fruit), but it still holds a special place in my heart. This cheesecake showcases it in all its glory, complemented by spicy ginger and sweet, rich and creamy chocolate cheesecake. It's definitely worth the faff – just make sure you have a sharp knife! * *makes a 20cm (8in) cheesecake*

*For the base*

75g (¾ cup) ground almonds
50g (½ cup) desiccated coconut
85g (½ cup) coconut sugar
70g (⅓ cup) coconut oil, plus extra for greasing
1 teaspoon ground ginger

*For the filling*

195g (1½ cups) cashews, soaked in
  water for at least 2 hours
120g (½ cup) coconut cream
80g (¼ cup) pure maple syrup
3 tablespoons coconut oil
125ml (½ cup) coconut yogurt
25g (¼ cup) cacao powder
1 tablespoon lemon juice
pinch of Himalayan salt

*To decorate*

pulp of 2 passion fruits
35g (¼ cup) chocolate chunks (vegan
  store-bought or make your own, see page 21)

1. Preheat your oven to 180°C/gas mark 4.

2. Combine the ingredients for the base in a food processor. Whizz until combined and press this into a greased 20cm (8in) tart tin.

3. Bake for around 10 minutes or until the base begins to turn golden. Don't worry if it's not hard when you remove it from the oven as it will be baked again once the filling has gone on top.

4. Place the filling ingredients in a food processor and blend until smooth. Pour this into the base and bake for around 20 minutes. Leave it to cool and then place in the fridge for 2 to 3 hours to firm up.

5. Spread the passion fruit on top, then melt the chocolate in a bowl over a saucepan half-full with water on a low heat, making sure the bowl is not touching the water. Remove from the heat and drizzle over the cheesecake.

# CHOC TARTS

NUT-FREE

My parents never allowed me to have toaster pastries for breakfast, understandably so, because looking back they were definitely on the less healthy side of the breakfast offerings available. But once I got my hands on them, blown away was I. Pop them in the toaster and out they came, all gooey on the inside and crunchy but also chewy on the outside. I mean, what's not to like? This version doesn't require toasting, but they're just as tasty and a lot less unhealthy! My daughter loved them so much after I tested them for this book, she's not stopped badgering me to make them since – I suppose the circle is now complete!
*makes around 4 pop tarts*

> 90g (1 cup) ground oats
> 60g (½ cup) buckwheat flour
> 2 tablespoons cacao powder
> pinch of Himalayan salt
> 50g (¼ cup) coconut oil, melted
> 80g (¼ cup) pure maple syrup
> 1 teaspoon vanilla extract
> ½ batch of my chocolate spread (see page 14)

1. Mix the first four ingredients in a bowl, then add in the other ingredients, except the chocolate spread, and knead into a dough.

2. Roll the dough on floured baking paper until it is around 3mm (0.1in) thick, then pop it in the fridge for around 15 minutes.

3. Cut the dough into eight rectangles and place the chocolate spread onto half of them, leaving a little room around the edges. Place the other rectangles on top and seal by pressing down with the prongs of a fork all around the edges.

4. Bake at 180°C/gas mark 4 for 10 minutes, then leave to cool slightly before eating.

5. Store in an airtight container for up to 5 days.

# AZTEC CHOCOLATE TART

It seemed only right to include a nod to the Aztecs, as they really were cacao OGs. They used cacao beans as currency way back in the fifteenth century and they believed that chocolate was a gift from the gods, which I am inclined to agree with. They drank hot chocolate (*xocolatl*) as an aphrodisiac and even to prepare for war. They also enjoyed it with a little kick of chilli, a spot of cinnamon and a hint of vanilla. I incorporated these flavours into a tart and I'm pretty sure the ancient Aztecs would be all over it if they had a slice! *makes an 20cm (8in) tart*

> *For the base*
> 200g (2 cups) ground almonds
> 35g (⅓ cup) cacao powder
> 110g (⅓ cup) pure maple syrup
> 2 tablespoons coconut oil, melted

> *For the filling*
> ¾ x 400ml can full-fat coconut milk (300ml)
> 140g (1 cup) chocolate chunks (vegan store-bought or make your own, see page 21)
> 1 tablespoon ground cinnamon
> 1 teaspoon vanilla extract
> ½ teaspoon mild chilli powder
> Himalayan salt, to sprinkle

1. Put the ingredients for the base in a bowl and mix until combined, then press evenly into a 20cm (8in) greased tart tin on the base and sides.

2. Place the coconut milk in a bowl over a saucepan half-full of water on a medium heat, until it starts to bubble a little. Remove from the heat, add in the chocolate and cover for 5 minutes.

3. Stir in the chocolate, then add in the cinnamon, vanilla and chilli and stir again. Pour this onto the base and place in the fridge for 3 hours to set.

4. Sprinkle salt on top to serve. Store for up to 5 days in the fridge or freeze for up to 2 months.

# TO MARS AND BACK CHEESECAKE

One of my daughter's favourite things is space. I'll often find her poring over one of her space books and, as such, she has a wealth of knowledge on the subject. She does still have some questions though . . .
How do astronauts go to the toilet in space? Why can't we travel to the Sun?

So, this recipe is dedicated to her – it's big and round-shaped like the planet, it's got a rocky crust and it disappears faster than you can say 'total eclipse'. It's also got a nougat layer, with a caramel layer on top, all finished with a chocolatey shell. You could say it's out of this world!

*makes a 20cm (8in) cheesecake*

### For the base
195g (1½ cups) cashews
150g (1 cup) Medjool dates
1 tablespoon coconut oil

### Chocolate nougat cheesecake layer
195g (1½ cups) cashews, soaked in hot water for 2 hours
60g (¼ cup) cacao butter
6 tablespoons oat milk
5 tablespoons pure maple syrup
25g (¼ cup) cacao powder
1 teaspoon vanilla extract

### Caramel layer
75g (½ cup) Medjool dates
120g (½ cup) cashew butter
3 tablespoons coconut oil, melted
80ml (⅓ cup) oat milk
pinch of Himalayan salt

### Chocolate topping
60g (¼ cup) cacao butter
2 tablespoons pure maple syrup
3 tablespoons cacao powder

1. To make the base, put the cashews, dates and coconut oil in a food processor and blend until crumbly, then press into the base of a lined 20cm (8in) cake tin or pie dish and make sure it is evenly covered.

2. For the cheesecake layer, drain the cashews then blitz them in a high-speed blender or food processor. Melt the cacao butter in a bowl over a saucepan half-full of water on a low heat, making sure the bowl is not touching the water, then add to the blitzed cashews, along with the other cheesecake ingredients, and blend until it becomes a smooth, thick mixture. Spoon this on top of the base and place the cake in the freezer to set while you make the caramel.

3. Blend the caramel ingredients until smooth, then spoon this on top of the cheesecake layer, making sure it is evenly distributed. Place back in the freezer.

4. To make the chocolate topping, melt the cacao butter in a bowl over a saucepan half-full of water on a low heat, making sure the bowl is not touching the water, then stir in the maple syrup and cacao powder. Pour this on top of the caramel, then place it back in the freezer for 2 hours to allow it to set.

5. Remove from the freezer and allow to stand for 10 minutes before slicing and serving. Store in the fridge for up to 3 days or freeze for up to 2 months.

# CHOCOLATE COCONUT CHEESECAKE JARS

In the year where everything was cancelled, out of necessity we had a lot of picnics. A lot of soggy, chilly picnics. Whereas normally we'd have family over and I'd serve up all the desserts, I had to think fast and adjust to the new normal. I needed something portable that could be individually served too. Enter the cheesecake jar. These were an instant hit, just BYOS (bring your own spoon) and dig in. They are so easy to make and they look very fancy at the same time too. Chocolate and coconut together are always a good idea, and these are the perfect way to enjoy them, whether you're eating them al fresco or indoors! * *makes 4 small jars*

*For the crumb base*
50g (½ cup) walnuts
50g (½ cup) ground almonds
25g (¼ cup) cacao powder
3 tablespoons pure maple syrup
2 tablespoons coconut oil, melted

*For the cheesecake layer*
65g (½ cup) cashews, soaked in
   hot water for 2 hours
3 tablespoons pure maple syrup
125ml (½ cup) full-fat coconut milk
50g (½ cup) desiccated coconut,
   plus extra to decorate

*For the chocolate ganache topping*
2 tablespoons coconut oil
2 tablespoons pure maple syrup
2 tablespoons cacao powder
1 tablespoon coconut milk

1. In a food processor, whizz the walnuts, ground almonds and cacao until they have a crumb-like texture, then add in the maple syrup and coconut oil and blend for a further 10 seconds to combine. Spoon this into the base of four small jars and set aside.

2. To make the cheesecake layer, drain the cashews then blend them with the maple syrup and coconut milk until smooth. Stir in the desiccated coconut and spoon this on top of the bases. Place the cheesecakes in the freezer for half an hour to set.

3. For the topping, melt the coconut oil in a bowl over a saucepan half-full of water on a low heat, making sure the bowl is not touching the water, then remove from the heat and stir in the other ingredients. Spoon this on top of the cheesecakes and garnish with a little extra coconut.

4. Store in the fridge for up to 5 days or freeze for up to 2 months.

## Top tip
Although I use tasteless coconut oil for most recipes, I prefer the unrefined stuff for this as it adds to the lovely Bounty-like flavour!

# CHOCOLATE ORANGE TORTE

Chocolate torte was often on the menu for Friday night dinners when I was a teenager. It was so rich and decadent that between my family we could never quite finish it, so I'd often treat myself to a little slice of the leftovers with my Saturday morning breakfast. Those days feel like a distant memory: sleeping in until late in the morning, lounging around, then going out on a Saturday night at the time when these days I'm going to bed (and sometimes not returning until the time I now get woken up!) but the torte love is very much still the same. A little orange zest balances out the sweet, rich chocolatey flavour. It's so good that there's never any left for my breakfast when I make it these days!

\* *makes a 20cm (8in) torte*

*For the base*
160g (1¾ cups) ground oats
35g (⅓ cup) cacao powder
80g (¼ cup) pure maple syrup
2 tablespoons coconut oil, melted, plus extra for greasing
pinch of Himalayan salt

*For the torte*
240g (1⅓ cups) chocolate chunks (vegan store-bought or make your own, see page 21)
2 tablespoons pure maple syrup
480g (2 cups) coconut cream
80ml (⅓ cup) aquafaba (chickpea water from a can of chickpeas)
3 tablespoons cacao powder, plus extra for dusting
zest of 1 orange, plus slices to decorate

**NUT-FREE**

1. Combine the ingredients for the base in a bowl and mix well, then knead into a dough and press down into the base of a greased 20cm (8in) tart or cake tin.

2. Put the chocolate in a bowl over a saucepan half-full of water, making sure the bowl is not touching the water, and heat on a low heat, stirring until melted. Add in the maple syrup and half of the coconut cream, then stir well and remove from the heat.

3. Add the rest of the coconut cream and the aquafaba to a stand mixer and whisk on high for around 10 minutes until it has thickened up.

4. Add the chocolate mixture as well as the cacao into the stand mixer and mix on high until combined. Finally, stir in the orange zest and mix well.

5. Pour the mixture into your cake tin and place in the freezer for an hour to set. Dust with a little extra cacao powder, decorate with the orange and slice to serve.

6. Store in the fridge for up to 3 days or freeze for up to 2 months.

## Top tip

To dust the cacao evenly, place a spoonful of it in a small sieve and tap the sieve lightly over the torte. For extra snazzy presentation, cut out a design from a piece of paper and place it over the cake before dusting, so that once removed, it leaves an undusted design!

There's a lot of magic in this chapter, in fact these recipes are nothing short of enchanted. I've included my go-to birthday cake, fit for a prince or princess, which I have made so many times that if I was Sleeping Beauty I could probably make it for the seven dwarves whilst catching forty winks. You'll also find a beautiful marble cake, a toffee cake which oozes caramel as you cut into it, like a cake piñata, and mug cakes that are quicker to make than it takes Rapunzel to let down her hair.

All sorts of secret ingredients seem to have snuck into these pages too. I mean, if a fairy godmother can make carriages out of pumpkins, then I can makes cakes out of carrots, courgettes and sweet potatoes, to name but a few. Just call me CinderEmma.

Chapter 5

*

# CAKES & LOAVES

# YOLO TOFFEE CAKE

For anyone who isn't familiar with the term, 'YOLO' stands for 'you only live once'. It makes me cringe a little when people say it, so believe me when I'm talking in jest (or is that ingest?). But life is too short to eat average cake. Enter my YOLO toffee cake. Not only is the cake super chocolatey and wonderful, but there's a secret caramel filling, like a cake piñata if you will. Add to that a chocolate coating and we're headed into the realms of cake euphoria.

* *makes a 3-layer 15cm (6in) cake*

### For the cake

70g (⅔ cup) ground almonds
40g (⅓ cup) buckwheat flour
100g (1 cup) cacao powder
pinch of Himalayan salt
60g (¼ cup) cashew butter
320g (1 cup) pure maple syrup
250ml (1 cup) oat milk
2 flax eggs (2 tablespoons ground flaxseeds left with 6 tablespoons water in a bowl for 5 minutes to thicken)
coconut oil, for greasing

### For the caramel filling

160g (½ cup) pure maple syrup
125ml (½ cup) full-fat coconut milk
pinch of Himalayan salt

### For the ganache filling and coating

105g (¾ cup) chocolate chunks (vegan store-bought or make your own, see page 21)
6 tablespoons full-fat coconut milk

## Top tip

Use the leftover cut-out cake as a layer for my peanut butter chocolate trifles on page 150!

1. To make the cake, preheat your oven to 180°C/gas mark 4.

2. Place the ground almonds, buckwheat flour, cacao powder and salt in a stand mixer or bowl and whisk until combined (or mix by hand).

3. Put the cashew butter, maple syrup and oat milk in another bowl and stir well, then add this and the flax eggs to the dry ingredients and mix until well combined.

4. Spoon this mixture into three 15cm (6in) cake tins greased with coconut oil, then bake for 25 minutes or until a skewer inserted comes out clean. The cakes are quite fudgy, so don't worry if they still seem quite soft when they come out! Place them on a cooling rack to cool.

5. To make the caramel filling, put the maple syrup in a saucepan on a medium heat then, once it starts to bubble, add in the other ingredients and stir gently. Leave to simmer for around 15 minutes. Once it has started to thicken up, remove from the heat and leave to cool. Make sure you don't let it get too thick as it will thicken more while it cools – it should still run off your spoon a little when you remove it from the heat. It does need to be thick enough not to spill out of the cake when you cut into it though.

6. Cut out a circle from the middle of one of the cakes. Melt the chocolate in a bowl over a saucepan half-full of water on a low heat, making sure the bowl is not touching the water, then remove from the heat and stir in the coconut milk. Place this in the fridge for half an hour to harden up, then spread a layer onto one of the uncut cakes and place the cake with a circle cut out on top.

7. Spoon the caramel into the middle of the cut cake, then spread more ganache on this cake and place the third cake on top. Spread the rest of the ganache on top of the cake and round the sides to make it into a giant toffee cake!

8. Store in the fridge for up to 5 days or in the freezer for up to 2 months.

# MY GO-TO BIRTHDAY CAKE

Despite the fact that creating new recipes is very much my (gluten-free) bread and (vegan) butter, there are some tried-and-tested ones that I go back to again and again. This is very true for birthday cakes, both for my little ones and for my cake customers, because I need to know that what I'm baking is going to come out delicious every single time. I have lost count of the number of times I've made this cake, but it must be in the hundreds, if not thousands.

I sandwich layers of this decadent chocolate fudge cake with my chocolate ganache on page 22, then decorate to my heart's desire with all the bars, balls and chocolates!
✳ *makes one 20cm (8in) cake*

### For the cake
150g (1 cup) Medjool dates
100g (1 cup) cacao powder
7 tablespoons cashew butter
100g (½ cup) coconut oil
9 tablespoons pure maple syrup
50g (½ cup) ground almonds
180ml (¾ cup) almond milk
1 batch of my milk chocolate ganache (see page 22)

1.  Preheat your oven to 180°C/gas mark 4.

2.  Place all the ingredients, except the ganache, in a food processor and blend for around 2 minutes until smooth. Spoon the mixture into a lined 20cm (8in) cake tin and bake for 25 minutes. Leave to cool while you make the ganache.

3.  Make the ganache as per the instructions on page 22, then spoon or pipe this onto the cake.

4.  Store in the fridge for up to 5 days or freeze for up to 2 months.

### Top tip
I like adding all the treats on top: different-flavoured balls, brownie chunks and homemade chocolates, but if you haven't any of these to hand, a selection of berries looks very fancy and adds a pop of colour!

# SNEAKY BANANA BREAD

My best friend and I have only really ever disagreed on one thing – bananas. She claims she needs to eat a banana a day or she gets cramp, whereas I can't bear eating them 'on the rocks'. My daughter can easily get through five bananas a day if left unattended at a fruit bowl, but it turns out my older son is the same as me. But this banana bread has him fooled. He thinks he's hit the chocolate cake jackpot whenever I bake it and scoffs it down without question. It's the perfect combination of a classic banana bread but taken to the next level with a hint of chocolate. Perfect for a teatime treat with friends, and a delicious way to ward away those pesky cramps. ✳ *makes 1 loaf*

90g (1 cup) ground oats
100g (1 cup) ground almonds (sub
   with ground oats to make nut-free)
25g (¼ cup) cacao powder
3 very ripe medium bananas
80ml (⅓ cup) rapeseed oil
110g (⅓ cup) pure maple syrup
70g (½ cup) chocolate chunks (vegan
   store-bought or make your own, see page 21)

1. Preheat your oven to 180°C/gas mark 4.

2. Place the ground oats, ground almonds, cacao powder in a bowl and stir.

3. In a separate bowl, mash the bananas well and then stir in the rapeseed oil and maple syrup.

4. Pour this mixture into the dry ingredients and mix until well combined, then stir in the chocolate chunks.

5. Spoon the mixture into a lined baking loaf tin or mould and bake for 25–30 minutes until a skewer inserted comes out clean.

6. Leave to cool before slicing and store in an airtight container in the fridge or freezer.

# CHOCOLATE SWISS ROLL

I've never been to Switzerland, but I like the way they roll. I remember being totally obsessed with the little mini chocolate Swiss rolls you could get from the supermarket when I was younger. Eating them was like a ritual: I'd eat all the chocolate from around the outside first, then I'd nibble away at the sponge spiral with its swirl of filling inside, every bite tasting like absolute heaven.

I'm not sure why they are called Swiss rolls, as apparently they were invented in Austria, but history aside, these are in fact very easy to put together. Once you've rolled up your Swiss roll you can cover it in chocolate, and it makes for a great Yule log at Christmas time too! If you don't want to fill the roll with ganache, you could use jam instead or even a nut butter. I've a few little tricks up my sleeve as well to make sure your cake rolls up nicely – it's genius if I do say so myself!

✱ *serves 8–10*

1 teaspoon apple cider vinegar
250ml (1 cup) oat milk
100g (1 cup) porridge oats
70g (⅔ cup) cacao powder
40g (¼ cup) cornflour
170g (1 cup) coconut sugar
120g (½ cup) cashew butter (or tahini to make it nut-free)
50g (¼ cup) coconut oil, melted

## For the ganache filling
½ batch of my chocolate recipe (see page 21)
60g (¼ cup) coconut cream

## For the coating
½ batch of my chocolate recipe (see page 21)

1. Preheat your oven to 180°C/gas mark 4. Put the vinegar and oat milk in a bowl and stir to make a vegan buttermilk.

2. Add the oats, cacao powder, cornflour and coconut sugar to a food processor and whizz to form a flour.

3. Whisk the cashew butter and coconut oil into the buttermilk mixture, then sift in the flour mixture and gently whisk until just combined.

4. Spoon the batter into a lined 20cm (8in) square baking tin, then bake for 20 minutes. It may not seem fully cooked, but if left too long it will crack whilst rolling.

5. Leave to cool for 5 minutes, then place it on a sheet of baking paper and roll it up into a spiral shape using the baking paper (in the same way you'd use a sushi mat to roll up a sushi roll) whilst you make the filling. Don't worry if it cracks a little as you can always fill this in with some of the chocolate.

6. Prepare the filling by melting the chocolate in a bowl over a saucepan half-full with water on a low heat, making sure the bowl is not touching the water, then remove from the heat and stir in the coconut cream. Place in the fridge to set.

7. Once the filling is firm, place the cake on a sheet of baking paper, unroll and spread the filling on top, leaving an inch empty around the edges. Roll it up again, trimming the ends if necessary. Place in the freezer for half an hour as this will enable the coating to stick better.

8. Make the chocolate as per the instructions on page 21, then leave it to cool for 10 minutes as this will make it set quicker on the cake.

9. Unroll the cake from the baking paper, place it on a cooling rack, then pour the chocolate mixture over the cake slowly to cover it.

10. Place the cake in the fridge for half an hour to allow the chocolate to set then serve. Store in the fridge for up to 3 days or freeze for up to 2 months.

# BLACK FOREST GATEAU

The Black Forest (which upon searching online I discovered is in Germany – my geography knowledge is embarrassingly bad) sounds like my kind of forest. I can only imagine that it's the sort of place where all the trees are made of delicious chocolate cake, covered with cherries and cream in place of leaves, and where it rains not water, but chocolate shavings instead.

I was about to book a one-way ticket there but decided to do a little image search first. To my absolute dismay, the Black Forest looks like, well, just your average forest. Just like when we went to Jaffa and didn't see any oranges, let alone a cake, or when we went to New York, AKA the Big Apple, and all the fruit looked regular-sized.

So, to console myself, I came up with this cake. It's got a chocolatey sponge with creamy coconut and a tart, sweet cherry filling. The only way this cake could be better is if it grew on trees; that really would be a case of having our cake and eating it too.
* makes a 2-layer 15cm (6in) cake

100g (1 cup) porridge oats
100g (1 cup) cacao powder
60g (½ cup) buckwheat flour
70g (⅓ cup) coconut oil
2 chia eggs (2 tablespoons chia seeds left with 6 tablespoons water in a bowl for 5 minutes to thicken)
300ml (1¼ cups) oat milk
150g (1 cup) Medjool dates, pitted
80g (¼ cup) pure maple syrup
140g (1 cup) frozen cherries, plus extra to decorate

*For the cherry filling*
70g (½ cup) frozen cherries
2 tablespoons chia seeds
3 tablespoons pure maple syrup

*To finish*
120g (½ cup) coconut cream
2 tablespoons pure maple syrup
35g (¼ cup) raw chocolate, for shavings (optional)

1. Preheat your oven to 180°C/gas mark 4.

2. Whizz the oats in a high-speed blender for 30 seconds or so until they become a flour.

3. Combine the cacao powder, oat flour and buckwheat flour in a bowl and mix together, then place in a food processor with all the other cake ingredients except the cherries. Blend for around 2 minutes, then stir in the frozen cherries. Spoon the mixture into two 15cm (6in) lined cake tins and bake for 25 minutes.

4. To make the cherry filling, blend the ingredients in a food processor for a minute until smooth. Place in a saucepan and bring to the boil, then reduce the heat and simmer for 10 minutes, stirring regularly.

5. Let the mixture cool, then once the cakes have completely cooled, spread the cherry filling on one of the cakes.

6. Place the coconut cream and maple syrup in a bowl and stir well, then spoon this on top of the cherry filling. Sandwich the other cake on top and decorate with any extra cherries and chocolate shavings.

# MOCHA CHOCA LATTE YAYA CAKE

I was enamoured with the film *Moulin Rouge* when it came out, especially the version of the song 'Lady Marmalade' that was released for the soundtrack. I'd sing along, having no idea what '*Voulez-vous coucher avec moi ce soir,*' actually meant, or any of the lyrics. But as a chocolate and coffee lover, the thought of a 'mocha choca latte yaya' sounds pretty delicious to me, I mean, what's not to like? So, if you like your men (or women) like you like your coffee, ie rich, intense and sweet, then this is the cake for you.

I've used walnuts in this cake as everyone knows coffee and walnuts work together so very nicely! Coffee is also used in many chocolate cakes to bring out the chocolate flavour, and it really does exactly that! ✳
*makes a 2-layer 15cm (6in) cake*

180ml (¾ cup) almond milk
1 tablespoon apple cider vinegar
60ml (¼ cup) rapeseed oil
10 tablespoons pure maple syrup
1 teaspoon vanilla extract
125ml (¼ cup) strong brewed coffee
125g (1¼ cups) ground walnuts
75g (¾ cup) cacao powder
60g (½ cup) buckwheat flour
30g ( (¼ cup) chopped walnuts

## For the frosting
½ the hard part of a can of full-fat
   coconut milk, refrigerated
2 tablespoons pure maple syrup
1 teaspoon vanilla extract
1 tablespoon espresso coffee

1. Preheat your oven to 180°C/gas mark 4.

2. Place the almond milk and vinegar in a bowl, stir gently and leave to sit for 5 minutes, then add in the rapeseed oil, maple syrup, vanilla and coffee and stir to mix.

3. In another bowl, sift together the ground walnuts, cacao powder and buckwheat flour, then pour in the wet ingredients and stir until just combined.

4. Fold in the chopped walnuts, then transfer the mixture to two lined 15cm (6in) cake tins and bake for around 20 minutes or until an inserted skewer comes out clean. Leave to cool completely before frosting.

5. To make the frosting, spoon the hardened part of the coconut milk into a bowl along with the other ingredients (except the liquid from the can of coconut milk), then whisk with a stand or hand mixer to fluff up the cream a little.

6. Place the frosting in the fridge for half an hour to chill, then pop one of the cakes on a plate and spread half the frosting evenly on top. Sandwich the second cake on top and repeat with the remaining frosting.

7. Store in an airtight container in the fridge for up to 3 days or freeze for up to 2 months.

## Top tip
The liquid from the can is coconut water, so use it in a smoothie instead of throwing it away!

# MATCHA CHOCOLATE AND ALMOND CAKE

My favourite part of the week happens on a Saturday morning; the boys go to football class and my daughter Azaria and I go and get a hot drink before her ballet lesson. I soak up every second of that time, chatting to her about life and school and whatever is on her mind, wishing she could stay small forever. This cake is inspired by our café orders: I get a matcha latte with almond milk and she gets a hot chocolate. She drinks hers as quickly as she possibly can; I sip and savour mine whilst I answer questions fired at me ten to the dozen.

Whether you are a scoffer or a savourer, this cake is so full of flavours. Bright, earthy matcha works so well with light vanilla and almonds, topped off with a sweet, rich chocolatey filling and frosting.
* *makes a 20cm (8in) cake*

1 teaspoon apple cider vinegar
250ml (1 cup) almond milk
270g (2⅔ cups) ground almonds
2 tablespoons matcha powder
50g (¼ cup) coconut oil, melted
120g (½ cup) almond butter
1 teaspoon vanilla extract
160g (½ cup) pure maple syrup

*For the chocolate filling and frosting*
120g (½ cup) almond butter
50g (¼ cup) pure maple syrup
25g (¼ cup) cacao powder
3 tablespoons almond milk
pinch of Himalayan salt

1. Preheat your oven to 180°C/gas mark 4.

2. Pour the apple cider vinegar and almond milk into a bowl, stir and set aside.

3. In another bowl, stir the ground almonds and matcha powder to mix together.

4. Add the coconut oil, almond butter, vanilla and maple syrup to the other wet ingredients and stir to combine, before making a well in the dry ingredients and stirring in the wet mixture.

5. Pour this into two 20cm (8in) cake tins and bake for 25 minutes or until an inserted skewer comes out clean. Leave to cool while you make the frosting and filling.

6. Add the frosting and filling ingredients to a bowl and stir until smooth and chocolatey. Spread half on one of the cakes, place the other on top and spread the rest of the filling on top of that.

7. Store in the fridge for up to 5 days or freeze for up to 2 months.

# CHOCOLATE AND TAHINI MARBLE CAKE

Apparently, marble cakes originated in nineteenth-century Germany, where they marbled spices and molasses into their cakes. The recipe then made its way over to America via the immigrants that relocated there, and the first recipe recorded there is a Jewish recipe featuring chocolate marbled in the cake. I've also used tahini in this recipe; its flavour works so well and it makes the cake lovely and moist. ✳ *makes 1 loaf*

> 200g (2 cups) ground almonds
> 60g (½ cup) buckwheat flour
> 130g (¾ cup) coconut sugar
> 100g (½ cup) coconut oil, melted
> 80g (⅓ cup) applesauce
> 60g (¼ cup) tahini
> 310ml (1¼ cups) almond milk, at room temperature
> 25g (¼ cup) cacao powder

1.  Preheat your oven to 180°C/gas mark 4. Mix the ground almonds, buckwheat flour and coconut sugar in a bowl.

2.  In another bowl, stir together the coconut oil, applesauce, tahini and 250ml (1 cup) of the almond milk until well combined. Pour this into the dry ingredients and stir to combine.

3.  Spoon one half of the mixture into another bowl and add the cacao powder and remaining almond milk.

4.  In a lined baking loaf tin, dollop alternate spoonfuls of each mixture, then take a skewer or chopstick and swirl the batter around to create a marbled effect.

5.  Bake for 60 minutes or until a skewer inserted comes out clean. Leave to cool before serving. Store in an airtight container in the fridge for a week or freeze for up to 2 months.

## Top tip
To make applesauce, blend an apple until it forms a purée.

# 5-MINUTE MUG CAKES

I feel like a fully-fledged magician pulling a rabbit out of a hat when I remove these bad boys from the microwave. I was never good at chemistry at school; my experiments always seemed to go wrong and they once had to evacuate the entire laboratory mid-class after I dropped a mercury thermometer on the floor. However, when I make these mug cakes, I feel like I'm doing some sort of magic science experiment. Just a few ingredients mixed up, a minute to cook and all the molten chocolatey mug cake deliciousness is ready to eat. They're perfect for people like my kids (and me) who are quite impatient when it comes to dessert, although be sure to blow on the spoon if you're eating them straight away! ✳ *serves 2*

> 2 tablespoons coconut oil
> 50g (½ cup) cacao powder
> 35g (⅓ cup) ground almonds
> pinch of Himalayan salt
> 5 tablespoons pure maple syrup
> 125ml (½ cup) almond milk
> 2 tablespoons peanut butter

1.  Place the coconut oil in a microwaveable bowl and microwave for 60 seconds to melt it.

2.  Add the cacao powder, ground almonds and salt to a mixing bowl and stir together well, before adding in the coconut oil and the rest of the wet ingredients. Mix well until you have a smooth cake mixture.

3.  Spoon the mixture into two ramekins or small mugs and microwave on high (1000W) for 3 minutes. Grab a spoon and enjoy!

# SUPER-SECRET CHOCOLATE SALAD CAKE

They say you don't make friends with salad. Well, I beg to differ. I love making big salads, especially in the summertime, with loads of avocado, all the roasted vegetables, toasted nuts, dried fruit and a sweet tangy dressing. I thought it would be fun to create a cake with all my favourite salad elements in it – and it turned out so well! It's secretly packed with veggies, fibre and healthy fats and very, very tasty! My kids loved this cake – little did they know what had gone into it!

✱ *makes a 15cm (6in) cake*

*For the cake*
½ medium sweet potato, peeled and
    chopped into chunks
½ ripe medium avocado
100g (1 cup) ground almonds
30g (¼ cup) buckwheat flour
60g (¼ cup) tahini
75g (¾ cup) cacao powder
160g (½ cup) pure maple syrup
75g (½ cup) Medjool dates
60ml (¼ cup) light olive oil
35g (⅓ cup) walnuts

*For the frosting*
½ medium sweet potato
80g (¼ cup) pure maple syrup
25g (¼ cup) cacao powder

1.  Preheat your oven to 180°C/gas mark 4.

2.  Boil 1 medium sweet potato on a medium to high heat until soft, then drain and set aside, saving half of it for the frosting.

3.  Place all the cake ingredients except the walnuts in a food processor and whizz until combined. Add in the walnuts and pulse for 10 seconds, then spoon into a 15cm (6in) lined cake tin and bake for 25 minutes. Leave to cool before you make the frosting.

4.  Place the remaining sweet potato, maple syrup and cacao powder in a food processor and whizz until smooth, then spread this on top of the cake.

5.  Store the cake in the fridge for up to 5 days or freeze for up to 2 months.

# WHITE CHOC-FROSTED CARROT LOAF

As a lifetime chocoholic, it feels very weird to be professing my love for a cake named after a root vegetable, but goodness me, do I love a good carrot cake. Always have. Which could well explain why I've never needed a prescription for glasses, or perhaps not. Perhaps it's actually because during school/university/the office when I should have been squinting at textbooks or laptops, I was usually chatting to the long-suffering person next to me. But what I do know is that carrot cake and white chocolate make a perfect pairing. Don't get me wrong, I'm as big a cream-cheese frosting lover as they come, but the light sweet white chocolate smothered onto this loaf just works a real treat. Vegetables at their very best.

*makes 1 loaf*

## For the cake
175g (1¾ cups) porridge oats
50g (½ cup) walnuts
1 tablespoon ground cinnamon
1 ripe medium banana
125ml (½ cup) almond milk
110g (⅓ cup) pure maple syrup
60ml (¼ cup) rapeseed oil
5 medium carrots, chopped into chunks
80g (½ cup) raisins

## For the frosting
1 tablespoon cacao butter
2 tablespoons almond milk
1 tablespoon cornflour
2 tablespoons pure maple syrup
4 tablespoons cashew butter
1 teaspoon vanilla extract

1. Preheat your oven to 180°C/gas mark 4.

2. Blend the oats in a high-speed blender or food processor until they form a flour, then transfer them to a bowl and blend the walnuts for around 10 seconds to chop them into chunks. Add the walnuts and cinnamon to the oats.

3. Blend together the banana, almond milk, maple syrup, oil and the carrots. Pour this into the dry ingredients and mix well before folding in the raisins. Spoon the mixture into a lined baking loaf tin and bake for 30 minutes. Allow to cool completely before frosting.

4. Melt the cacao butter in a bowl over a saucepan half-full of water on a low heat, making sure the bowl is not touching the water, then set aside.

5. Put the almond milk and cornflour in a saucepan on a high heat and mix well. Bring to the boil and then remove from the heat and stir in the maple syrup, cashew butter, melted cacao butter and vanilla.

6. Place the frosting in the fridge for half an hour to set, then once the loaf is fully cooled, spread the frosting on top. Store in an airtight container in the fridge for up to 5 days or freeze for up to two months.

# FROSTED CHOCOLATE GINGER AND COURGETTE LOAF

I've always been really into fashion, and although these days I often end up choosing comfort over style (hashtag mum life), I still love poring over glossy magazines and window shopping in fancy department stores whenever I get the chance. One thing I've heard whispered about on the 'frow' recently is that courgette is the new carrot when it comes to baking. Not only can you get in some greens, but it also helps bakes from becoming too dry, and it pairs really well when you accessorise it with some cacao and a little ginger spice. Top it off with some chocolate frosting and you're looking at the chicest bake in town. * *Makes 1 loaf*

90g (1 cup) ground oats
40g (⅓ cup) buckwheat flour
50g (½ cup) cacao powder
1 teaspoon ground ginger
130g (¾ cup) coconut sugar
1 medium banana
150g (1 cup) grated courgette
6 tablespoons oat milk
6 tablespoons coconut oil, melted

## For the frosting
120g (½ cup) cashew butter (use tahini to make it nut-free)
25g (¼ cup) cacao powder
5 tablespoons oat milk
4 tablespoons pure maple syrup

1. Preheat your oven to 180°C/gas mark 4.

2. Put the ground oats, buckwheat flour, cacao powder, ground ginger and coconut sugar in a bowl and mix until combined.

3. Mash the banana in another bowl, then add in the courgette, oat milk and coconut oil and stir well. Add this to the dry mixture and mix again well, then spoon this into a lined baking loaf tin and bake for 30 minutes or until a skewer inserted comes out clean. Allow the loaf to cool while you make the frosting.

4. Mix the frosting ingredients together in a bowl, then pipe or spoon it on top of the loaf.

5. Store in an airtight container in the fridge for up to 5 days or freeze for up to 2 months.

I adore travelling. Mr H and I have been on so many wonderful adventures, and whilst they've definitely got less relaxing in recent years (*Kids on a Plane* would arguably make a scarier sequel to the film *Snakes on a Plane*) they've also got more fun. Foreign lands are also where I find some of the best inspiration for new creations in the kitchen. This chapter features many of these: hazelnut cookies and biscotti inspired by visits to Italy; cupcakes inspired by trips to the US; and the world's best choc-chip cookies inspired by, well, the world. Can I have that one?

But home is where the heart is, and it's also where my kitchen is, so at the end of every trip I'm always brimming with new ideas, excited to get baking delicious new things. Anything to put off all the unpacking and endless washing.

Chapter 6

*

# COOKIES, CUPCAKES & MUFFINS

# DEATH BY CHOCOLATE CUPCAKES

It seemed right to name these cupcakes as so as they're totally to die for – devilishly good and also rather heavenly at the same time. They are so chocolatey and indulgent and feature not only chocolate chips, but chocolate frosting on top as well. Some might call it chocolate overload, but I might call those people wrong. In fact, I could murder a few of these right now!

* *makes around 15 cupcakes*

## *For the cupcakes*
125g (1¼ cups) ground almonds
75g (¾ cup) plus 2 tablespoons cacao powder
120g (⅔ cup) coconut sugar
pinch of Himalayan salt
70g (⅓ cup) coconut oil, melted
240g (¾ cup) pure maple syrup
250ml (1 cup) oat milk
120g (½ cup) peanut butter
3 flax eggs (3 tablespoons ground flaxseeds left
    with 9 tablespoons water in a bowl for
    5 minutes to thicken)
140g (1 cup) chocolate chips

## *For the frosting*
½ a batch of my chocolate buttercream
    frosting (see page 20)

## *To decorate (optional)*
chocolate chips or cacao nibs

1. Preheat your oven to 180°C/gas mark 4.

2. To make the cupcakes, pop the ground almonds, cacao powder, coconut sugar and salt in a bowl and mix well.

3. In a separate bowl, stir together the melted coconut oil, maple syrup, oat milk, peanut butter and flax eggs until combined, then fold this into the dry ingredients. Finally, stir in the chocolate chips, then spoon the mixture into about 15 cupcake cases in a muffin tin and bake in the oven for 25 minutes. Leave to cool completely before adding the frosting.

4. Sppon frosting as per the instructions on page 20 and either spoon it on top or cut the end of a piping bag and inset an open-star nozzle. Spoon in the frosting, twist the bag tightly and apply pressure to push the frosting down. Place the bag vertically over your cupcake and, starting from the outside, work in a circle, spiralling into the centre as you continue to apply even pressure to squeeze out the frosting.

5. Repeat for all the cupcakes and decorate with any extras on top!

# WHITE CHOC CHEESECAKE BLUEBERRY STUFFINS

NUT-FREE

Blueberry muffins are, in my opinion, the OG of muffins. If muffin flavours were a category on *Family Fortunes*, blueberry would be right up there, and I'm pretty sure chocolate would be close behind it. Fortunately for you, I figured a way to get both flavours in one delicious invention – enter 'stuffins'. Aptly named because they are muffins with stuff in. These are light and fluffy on the outside with a very cheeky white chocolate cheesecake middle. I could ask for muffin more!

*✻ makes 8–10 muffins*

135g (1½ cups) ground oats
60g (½ cup) buckwheat flour
180g (¾ cup) applesauce (or around 2 apples puréed)
160g (½ cup) pure maple syrup
2 extra-ripe bananas, mashed
1½ teaspoons vanilla extract
150g (1 cup) fresh blueberries

### For the filling
2 tablespoons cacao butter
6 tablespoons vegan cream cheese
2 tablespoons pure maple syrup
1 teaspoon vanilla extract

1. Preheat your oven to 180°C/gas mark 4.

2. Put the oats and buckwheat flour in a bowl and stir well, before creating a well in the middle and stirring in the applesauce, maple syrup, bananas and vanilla.

3. Finally, fold in the blueberries, spoon the mixture into muffin cases on a muffin tray and bake for 25 minutes. Leave to cool then, using an apple corer, remove the centres from the stuffins.

4. Melt the cacao butter in a bowl over a saucepan half-full of water on a low heat, making sure the bowl is not touching the water, then stir in the other ingredients. Pipe this into the centre of the stuffins, using any leftover filling to frost the muffins on top.

5. Place them in the fridge for 10 minutes to allow the filling to harden. Store in the fridge for up to 5 days in an airtight container or freeze for up to 2 months.

## Top tip
If you don't have a piping bag, cut a small amount off the corner of a sandwich bag or similar and use this as a makeshift piping bag instead!

# CHOCOLATE CARAMEL CUPCAKES

A little salt really enhances the rich chocolatey flavour and helps to balance out the sweet. These cupcakes are so special as the caramel melts into the cupcake during cooking, and the frosting is so lovely and light on top. * *makes 10 cupcakes*

### For the cupcakes
30g (¼ cup) buckwheat flour
120g (⅔ cup) coconut sugar
75g (¾ cup) cacao powder
2 chia eggs (2 tablespoons chia seeds left
    with 6 tablespoons water in a bowl
    for 5 minutes to thicken)
60g (¼ cup) cashew butter
180ml (¾ cup) almond milk

### For the caramel and frosting
1 batch of my chocolate caramel (see page 22)
120g (½ cup) coconut cream

1. Preheat your oven to 180°C/gas mark 4.

2. Put the buckwheat flour, coconut sugar and cacao powder in a bowl and stir well.

3. In another bowl, mix together the chia eggs, cashew butter and almond milk until well combined, then create a well in the centre of the dry ingredients. Pour in the wet mixture and stir until just combined.

4. Spoon the mixture into 10 cupcake cases placed in a muffin tin, filling them two-thirds full.

5. Spoon half of the caramel over the cupcakes (around 1 heaped teaspoon per cake), then bake for 30 minutes. Leave to cool completely before making the frosting.

6. Whip the rest of the caramel with the coconut cream using a stand or hand mixer until fluffy, then place it in the fridge for an hour to set.

7. Spoon or pipe onto the cupcakes, then store in an airtight container in the fridge for up to a week.

# CHOCOLATE FOR BREAKFAST MUFFINS

**NUT-FREE**

Mr H and I are like two peas in a pod. We are both the world's biggest chocoholics and we'd eat chocolate at every meal if we could. When we go on holiday, he'll bypass all the hotel fry-up and pastry options and head straight for a bowl of Coco Pops (with almond milk, I've taught him well) and when we're at home, I make us smoothies with a little smidge of cacao powder, topped with chocolatey granola. Or if we're on the go, I make these. So easy to whip up a batch, and they'll last you all week! * *makes 9 muffins*

125g (1¼ cups) porridge oats
pinch of Himalayan salt
35g (⅓ cup) cacao powder
2 chia eggs (2 tablespoons chia seeds left
    with 6 tablespoons water in a bowl
    for 5 minutes to thicken)
160g (½ cup) pure maple syrup
80ml (⅓ cup) oat milk
1 medium banana, mashed (½ cup)
60ml (¼ cup) rapeseed oil
70g (½ cup) chocolate chunks (vegan
    store-bought or make your own, see page 21)
    or raisins

1. Preheat your oven to 160°C/gas mark 3.

2. In a bowl, mix together the oats, salt and cacao powder.

3. In another bowl, whisk together the chia eggs, maple syrup, oat milk, banana and rapeseed oil, then pour this into the dry ingredients and stir well, before folding in the chocolate chunks.

4. Spoon the mixture into muffin cases in a muffin tin and bake for 25 minutes or until an inserted skewer comes out clean.

5. Leave to cool, then store in an airtight container in the fridge for up to a week or freeze for up to 2 months.

# CHOCOLATE BABKA COOKIES

Babka, which actually means grandmother, is a traditional Jewish bake made with leftover challah bread dough, supposedly by grandmothers. I'd love to be able to tell you that this is a recipe passed down by my own grandma, but I don't think she ever baked a cake in her life. Hopefully though, I can pass this chocolatefied cookie version down to my children instead.

This looks very complicated with its swirled texture, but I'm here to show you that it's easier than it seems! I've made it into cookies as there's a lot of gluten and yeast in traditional babka loaves, so they are hard to replicate without these ingredients, as well as being quite time-consuming! So, these are my nod to the traditional version, no proofing or yeast needed! *makes 12 cookies*

*For the babka*

50ml (¼ cup) coconut oil, melted
6 tablespoons coconut sugar
60ml (¼ cup) oat milk
50g (½ cup) plus 2 tablespoons ground almonds
120g (1 cup) plus 2 tablespoons buckwheat flour, plus extra for dusting
1 tablespoon ground cinnamon
pinch of Himalayan salt
1–2 tablespoons water, plus more if needed

½ batch of my chocolate spread (see page 14) or any other chocolate spread

1. In a bowl, stir together the coconut oil, coconut sugar and oat milk and stir well.

2. In another bowl, combine the ground almonds, buckwheat flour, cinnamon and salt and mix together before folding into the wet mixture. Knead it for 5 minutes, adding in any water if needed, 1 tablespoon at a time, until you have a smooth and rollable dough.

3. Sprinkle a little buckwheat flour on your worktop, then roll the dough into a rectangle of around 5mm (0.2in) in thickness.

4. Spread the chocolate spread onto the dough and roll the dough up into a tube, placing the seam side down. Cut it in half lengthways with a serrated knife, then twist the two halves around each other as if making a two-piece plait.

5. Slice off the ends, then carefully slice the rest into 12 cookies. Place them lying down on a baking tray and bake at 180°C/gas mark 4 for 10 minutes.

6. Store in an airtight container at room temperature for up to a week.

## CHEWY CHUNKY COOKIES

**NUT-FREE** *option*

I used to think macadamia nuts were a joke from the universe. I'd pick up what looked like a delicious white chocolate cookie, take that first glorious bite, but the nutty realisation would have me crying into my skinny latte. Times, and I, have changed. I am now team macadamia; I love their light taste, their perfect texture, the list goes on. Their chunkiness works so well with sweet juicy cranberries and the cacao nibs that give it that perfect little hint of chocolate, whilst adding to the texture. If old me had picked up one of these cookies, I'm sure I wouldn't have been disappointed. * *makes 8 cookies*

> 50g (¼ cup) coconut oil
> 130g (¾ cup) coconut sugar
> 2 tablespoons oat milk
> 3 tablespoons tahini
> 1 teaspoon vanilla extract
> 100g (1 cup) porridge oats
> 40g (⅓ cup) buckwheat flour
> pinch of Himalayan salt
> 35g (¼ cup) macadamia halves (swap for extra dried fruit to make nut-free)
> 45g (⅓ cup) dried cranberries
> 4 tablespoons cacao nibs

1. Preheat your oven to 180°C/gas mark 4.

2. Put the coconut oil and coconut sugar in a stand mixer and whisk until combined. Add in the oat milk, tahini and vanilla and whisk again until incorporated, then add in the oats and buckwheat flour and whisk one more time. Once all combined, remove the bowl from the mixer and fold in the other ingredients.

3. Shape into about eight balls and place on a lined baking tray, then bake for 8 minutes. Leave to cool and then enjoy!

## CHOCCY BISCOTTI

I remember on trips to Italy receiving weird looks when I asked for a latte, so I just pointed at something and waited to see what I got. The tiniest little coffee in the tiniest little cup, with a biscuit on the side. Turns out that good things *do* come in small packages as that pairing was nothing short of mind-blowing. These days coffee sends me a little loopy, but I'm still here for all the biscuits. These biscotti are my version of that *bellissima* biscuit: crunchy, chocolatey and the perfect complement to any cuppa. * *makes 8 biscotti*

> 100g (1 cup) ground almonds
> 60g (½ cup) buckwheat flour
> 7 tablespoons coconut sugar
> 25g (¼ cup) cacao powder
> ½ teaspoon baking powder
> 2 tablespoons coconut oil, melted
> 80ml (⅓ cup) water
> 2 tablespoons cacao nibs

1. Preheat your oven to 180°C/gas mark 4.

2. In a bowl, mix together the ground almonds, buckwheat flour, coconut sugar, cacao powder and baking powder. Stir in the coconut oil and water, then stir in the cacao nibs.

3. Knead the dough, then shape it into a flat log around 7–8cm wide. Pop this on a lined baking tray and bake for 25 minutes, until the log feels firm.

4. Allow to cool, then refrigerate until cold. Using a sharp serrated knife, gently slice 1cm pieces.

5. Lay these on the baking tray again and bake at 120°C/gas mark ½ for 20 minutes, then turn and bake for another 20 minutes. Turn off your oven and leave them to cool in there for extra crunch!

6. Store in an airtight container at room temperature for up to a month.

# WHITE CHOCOLATE LEMON CUPCAKES

I love the fresh, tart flavour of lemon; it reminds me of accompanying my dad on his work trips to the US in the '90s, where my favourite thing to drink was (and still is) the fresh lemonade that we'd find being sold on street-corner kiosks. Mr H is a lemon lover too (when we first started living together back in 2011, we got through copious amounts of lemon squash), so I figured it would make sense to combine our favourite citrus fruit with another of our loves: chocolate. The light and sweet nature of white chocolate meant it was a no-brainer for these cupcakes as it works so well to balance out the zesty lemon.

*✳ makes 12 cupcakes*

### For the cupcakes
125ml (½ cup) oat milk
zest and juice from 1 lemon
125ml (½ cup) non-dairy yogurt
    (I like almond or coconut)
125ml (½ cup) rapeseed oil
200g (2 cups) ground almonds
60g (½ cup) buckwheat flour
130g (¾ cup) coconut sugar
pinch of Himalayan salt

### For the white chocolate frosting
60ml (¼ cup) oat milk
3 tablespoons pure maple syrup
3 tablespoons cacao butter
6 tablespoons coconut cream
6 tablespoons cashew butter
1 teaspoon vanilla extract

1.  Preheat your oven to 180°C/gas mark 4.

2.  Put the oat milk, lemon juice and zest in a bowl and stir, then add in the yogurt and rapeseed oil and stir gently to combine.

3.  In another bowl, stir together the other cupcake ingredients, then pour in the wet mixture and stir until just combined. Spoon into cupcake cases in a muffin tin and bake for 15 minutes, or until a skewer inserted into the centre of one of the cakes comes out clean. Leave to cool while you make the frosting.

4.  Place the oat milk and maple syrup in a saucepan and stir, then bring to a boil, remove from the heat and set aside.

5.  Place the cacao butter in a bowl and melt this over a saucepan half-full of water on a low heat, making sure the bowl is not touching the water.

6.  Whisk the coconut cream, cashew butter and vanilla with a stand or hand mixer, then add in the other frosting ingredients and continue to whisk until smooth. Place in the fridge to cool completely (it will harden up as it sets), then spoon it onto the cupcakes and serve.

7.  Store the cupcakes in an airtight container in the fridge for up to a week or freeze for up to 2 months.

# CHOCOLATE ORANGE COOKIE CUPS

Chocolate orange is one of my all-time favourite combinations as it takes me back to being little. These little cups are rather nifty, as they've got a crater in the middle, which is the perfect place to pop in extra chocolate orangey-ness. * *makes 6 cups*

70g (¾ cup) ground oats
50g (½ cup) ground almonds
25g (¼ cup) cacao powder
pinch of Himalayan salt
5 tablespoons pure maple syrup
60g (¼ cup) cashew butter
zest of ½ an orange
1–2 tablespoons water, plus more if needed

*For the filling*
2 tablespoons coconut oil, plus extra for greasing
1 tablespoon pure maple syrup
1 tablespoon cacao powder
1 tablespoon cashew butter
zest of ½ an orange
1 tablespoon cacao nibs

1. Preheat your oven to 180°C/gas mark 4. Mix the oats, ground almonds, cacao powder and salt in a bowl.

2. In another bowl, whisk the maple syrup, cashew butter and orange zest, then stir this into the dry ingredients to make a dough, adding in a little water a tablespoon at a time if necessary.

3. Split the dough into six balls, shape into cups, then lightly grease a muffin tin with coconut oil and add in the cups. Bake for 10 minutes and allow to cool before adding the filling.

4. For the filling, melt the coconut oil in a bowl over a saucepan half-full of water on a low heat, making sure the bowl is not touching the water. Remove from the heat and stir in the maple syrup, cacao powder and cashew butter. Add in the orange zest and cacao nibs, then spoon this into the centres of the cookie cups.

# ROOTIN' TOOTIN' BISCUIT SANDWICHES

A certain brand of wheel-shaped biscuits was so named to jump on the bandwagon of the popularity of Western movies. I'm not sure whether it was the promise of wheels made of cookies, or the idea of seeing a real-life cowboy, that led us to a Texas roadtrip with our friends back in the day, but my we had fun. One night culminated in the band who were playing in the only bar in town teaching us, the only non-locals, how to dance the two-step. Mr H swapped shirts with a man around 30 years his senior and we topped it off with a spot of drunk stargazing from our ranch. The wheels weren't edible, but it was an amazing trip nonetheless. These biscuits are my version, and they're rootin' tootin' good!

\* *makes around 5 biscuit sandwiches*

## For the biscuits

75g (¾ cup) ground almonds
60g (½ cup) buckwheat flour
pinch of Himalayan salt
50g (¼ cup) coconut oil, at
    room temperature
3 tablespoons pure maple syrup

## For the cream filling

3 tablespoons cacao butter
3 tablespoons coconut cream
2 tablespoons cashew butter
½ tablespoon pure maple syrup
½ teaspoon vanilla extract

100g (⅓ cup) sugar-free raspberry jam
½ a batch of my chocolate recipe
    (see page 21)

1. Preheat your oven to 180°C/gas mark 4.

2. In a bowl, mix together the ground almonds, buckwheat flour and salt. Cream in the coconut oil, and then add in the maple syrup. Leave the dough to chill in the fridge for 10 minutes, then roll it out to a thickness of about 5mm (0.2in) and use a cookie cutter or something circular to cut out circles.

3. Pop the biscuits on a lined baking tray and bake for 10–12 minutes.

4. While they are baking, melt the cacao butter in a bowl over a saucepan half-full of water on a low heat, making sure the bowl is not touching the water, then remove the bowl from the heat and stir in the other filling ingredients. Place the mixture in the freezer to chill while you wait for the biscuits.

5. Once the biscuits are baked, leave them to cool completely then refrigerate for 10 minutes before assembling, so that the fillings stick to them better.

6. Spoon around a teaspoon of the cream mixture onto half of the biscuits, then a teaspoon of jam onto the other half, then sandwich one of each half together. Place them in the freezer again while you make the chocolate as per the instructions on page 21.

7. Allow the melted chocolate to cool slightly, then dip each cookie in one by one, placing on a chopping board after each dip. Place them in the fridge to set, then enjoy!

8. Store in an airtight container in the fridge for up to 3 days.

# CHOC HAZELNUT-STUFFED COOKIES

These cookies have hazelnut chocolates to thank as their inspiration.
* *makes 6 cookies*

### For the chocolate filling
50g (¼ cup) coconut oil, melted
2 tablespoons cacao powder
2 tablespoons hazelnut butter
1½ tablespoons pure maple syrup
2 tablespoons toasted chopped hazelnuts
pinch of Himalayan salt

### For the cookies
75g (¾ cup) ground almonds
30g (¼ cup) buckwheat flour
50g (½ cup) plus 1 tablespoon cacao powder
5 tablespoons coconut sugar
1 tablespoon ground flaxseeds
pinch of Himalayan salt
60ml (¼ cup) almond milk
2 tablespoons hazelnut butter
2 tablespoons pure maple syrup

1. Preheat your oven to 180°C/gas mark 4. Combine the filling ingredients in a bowl and stir well until you have a thick mixture. Place the bowl in the fridge to set while you make the cookie mixture.

2. Put the ground almonds, buckwheat flour, cacao powder, coconut sugar, ground flaxseeds and salt in a large bowl and stir well before adding the other ingredients and stirring again until well combined.

3. Use half of the cookie batter to make six balls. Flatten these down one by one with your hands into cookies around 5mm (0.2in) thick and place them on a large baking sheet.

4. Evenly spoon the filling on top of the cookies, keeping it around 1cm clear of the edges. Make six more flat cookie shapes with the remaining batter and carefully place them on top, using your fingers to seal them down so that the filling can't escape.

5. Bake in the oven for 12 minutes, then leave to cool before digging in.

# CHOCAROONS

NUT-FREE

Welcome to Macaroon 101. Macaroons are made with almonds or coconut, Macarons are like meringue sandwiches. Macaroni is a type of pasta. The *Macarena* is a popular '90s song with some simple dance moves that if you grew up when I did, you'll have ingrained in your brain forever. But circling back to macaroons, these are typically eaten during the Jewish festival of Passover, so they're a little bit ingrained in me too. I've added extra chocolate for good measure because, to quote another song of that era, 'If you don't know me by now'! * *makes 8 macaroons*

110g (⅓ cup) pure maple syrup
125ml (½ cup) full-fat coconut milk
25g (¼ cup) cacao powder
pinch of Himalayan salt
170g (1⅘ cups) desiccated coconut
⅓ batch of my chocolate recipe (see page 21)

1. Preheat your oven to 160°C/gas mark 3.

2. Heat the maple syrup in a saucepan on a medium heat, then once it begins to boil, add the coconut milk and stir well. Remove from the heat and add in the cacao powder and salt, then stir in the coconut.

3. With an ice cream scoop or small cup, scoop up the mixture, compressing it into the scoop to make sure it is nice and compact, then place the semi-spheres on a lined baking tray.

4. Bake for around 25 minutes until they look toasted on top. Leave them to cool completely before coating in the chocolate.

5. Melt or make the chocolate as per the recipe on page 21, then dunk the bases of the macaroons in the chocolate mixture one by one.

6. Store in an airtight container in the fridge for up to a week.

# CHOCOLATE FIG BISCUITS

Every year, around the start of December, I start seeing figs on the supermarket shelves. But figs, like dogs, are not just for Christmas. Let's give figs the respect they deserve because they are delicious. Fresh ones in summer are a thing to behold, and dried figs in winter add the juiciest pop to everything from granola to puddings. These fig biscuits are fruity and cakey, with a hint of chocolate in the mix too. ✳ *makes 10–12 biscuits*

### For the biscuits
100g (1 cup) porridge oats
100g (1 cup) ground almonds
50g (¼ cup) coconut oil
80g (¼ cup) pure maple syrup
pinch of Himalayan salt

### For the filling
250g (1 cup) dried figs, stems removed
2 tablespoons cacao powder
½ teaspoon ground cinnamon
2 tablespoons coconut oil
4 tablespoons water

1. Preheat your oven to 180°C/gas mark 4. Whizz the biscuit ingredients in a food processor for around 2 minutes, until they form a smooth dough.

2. Roll this into a big ball and place it on a sheet of baking paper on a worktop. Roll out the mixture to a rectangle of around 1cm in thickness.

3. Blend the filling ingredients in a food processor and blend for around 5 minutes, until they form a sticky fig jam. Spoon this onto one half (lengthways) of your rectangle, leaving 1cm at each end.

4. Fold the non-jam-covered half over the jam-covered half to form a cylinder, then work the edges together with your hands to seal it. With a sharp knife, cut this into slices around 2cm thick, then place standing upright on a lined baking tray. Bake for 10 minutes, then leave to cool completely.

# THE WORLD'S BEST CHOC-CHIP COOKIES

These cookies are possibly the best I have ever made. Mr H said they tasted just like a regular cookie (you know, the ones packed with butter and gluten and all the stuff I don't eat) so that was a real win in my eyes. He certainly never lies when it comes to whether he likes my bakes or not as he's got no incentive to risk me baking something again that he pretended to like the first time! Anyway, I can't wait for you to try these cookies. They're just the right amount of sweet, gooey, crunchy, chocolatey and pretty perfect, if I do say so myself. ✳ *makes 10 cookies*

170g (1 cup) plus 3 tablespoons coconut sugar
pinch of Himalayan salt
2 tablespoons coconut oil, softened but not melted
5 tablespoons almond milk
60g (¼ cup) peanut butter
1 teaspoon vanilla extract
185g (1½ cups) flour (I use a mix of buckwheat flour, ground oats and ground almonds, but you can use a regular GF flour instead if you like!)
(1¼ cups) chocolate (about 200g), broken into chunks

1. Preheat your oven to 180°C/gas mark 4.

2. In a large bowl, mix together the coconut sugar, salt and coconut oil until combined. Add in the almond milk, peanut butter and vanilla until you have a smooth batter, then stir in the flour mix. Finally, stir in the chocolate chunks and split the dough into around 10 even-sized balls.

3. Place the balls on a lined baking tray, being sure to space them out so they have room to spread. Bake for 10–12 minutes, then leave to cool completely.

4. Store in an airtight container at room temperature for up to 2 weeks.

If the million-dollar question (on the gameshow *Who Wants to be a Millionaire Shortbread?*) was 'what are Emma's favourite desserts' and you answered 'anything baked in a tray' then you'd be right on the money. Not only do traybakes taste amazing, but there's no need for cutlery, or even a plate.

Having multiple children seems to involve saying the phrase 'sharing is caring' over and over but, I get it, sharing is tough. Which is another reason traybakes are so great, most of them can be cut into 16 little squares (or 9 big ones) so there's plenty to go around.

Many of these recipes call for a square tray; I use recyclable aluminium ones if I'm taking something with me somewhere, otherwise I use a lined square baking tray or silicone mould.

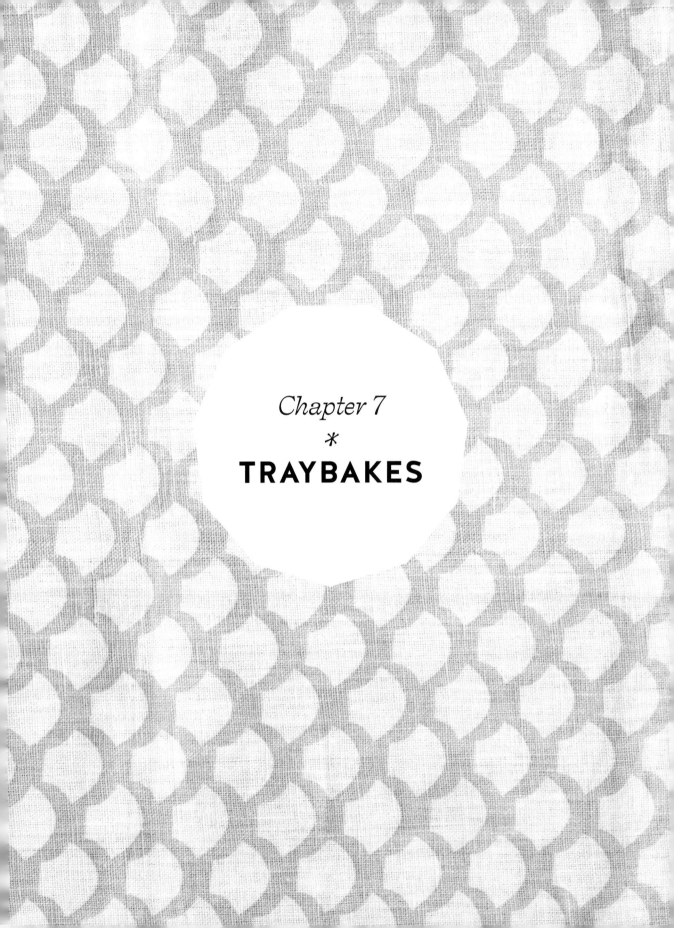

Chapter 7
*
# TRAYBAKES

# RED VELVET CHEESECAKE BROWNIES

I love everything about recipe creation, but the best bit for me (after the tasting) is being a recipe detective, delving into history. 'Velvet' was coined in the Victorian era, to inform lucky cake eaters that a bake would have a soft, smooth texture. This is because the cocoa would break down the coarse flour, and the cacao that they had at that time would give the cake a reddish hue. During 1940s rationing, people would use beetroot juice in their cakes to stop them from drying out, as well as mixing cream cheese with powdered sugar to form an easy tangy and sweet frosting. The cake went out of fashion until the 1989 film *Steel Magnolias* put it back on the map. Hence the name of the famous New York cake hotspot Magnolia Bakery! These brownies are so enticing, and the layers are the perfect complement to each other.

\* *makes a 20cm (8in) square tray-full*

### For the brownie layer

50g (¼ cup) coconut oil
60g (¼ cup) cashew butter
100g (1 cup) ground almonds
170g (1 cup) coconut sugar
50g (½ cup) cacao powder
pinch of Himalayan salt
125ml (½ cup) almond milk
2 tablespoons beetroot juice
1 teaspoon vanilla extract

### For the cheesecake layer

260g (2 cups) cashews,
    soaked in hot water
    for 2 hours
125ml (½ cup) almond milk
120g (½ cup) coconut cream
45g (¼ cup) coconut sugar
1 teaspoon lemon juice
1 teaspoon vanilla extract
pinch of Himalayan salt

1. Preheat your oven to 160°C/gas mark 3.

2. Add the ingredients for the brownies to a food processor and blend for around a minute until completely smooth, then spoon into a lined 20cm (8in) square baking tray or mould. Bake the brownie layer for 15 minutes, then leave to cool while you make the cheesecake layer.

3. Drain the cashews and add them and the other cheesecake ingredients to a food processor or high-speed blender, then blend until smooth. Spoon on top of the brownie mixture, then spread it out with the back of a spoon. Bake for 30 minutes, then allow to cool before cutting into slices.

4. Store in an airtight container in the fridge for up to a week or freeze for up to 2 months.

## Top tip

In my opinion, this one is best eaten chilled and straight from the fridge, so I like to leave it to cool in the refrigerator for a few hours before serving!

# TRIPLE-CHOCOLATE FROSTED HIDDEN AVOCADO BROWNIES

**NUT-FREE** *option*

I grew up reading the story about the baby who wouldn't eat anything apart from avocados and fully expected my children to like them once they started eating. Turns out 3/3 of them are not fans, which baffles me. I love the taste and the texture and all the healthy fats they provide are just an added bonus. Anyway, it turns out that avocado is the perfect secret ingredient in these brownies, as it gives them the most amazing texture and is a fantastic butter replacement. It works brilliantly in creating a creamy frosting too; delicious double avocado and my kids are none the wiser.

*✱ makes a 20cm (8in) square tray-full*

1. Preheat your oven to 170°C/gas mark 3.

2. Place the chocolate chunks in a bowl over a saucepan half-full of water, making sure the bowl is not touching the water, and heat on a low heat, stirring gently until melted.

3. While the chocolate is melting, halve, stone and scoop the flesh out of the avocado and place this and the rest of the brownie ingredients in a food processor. Whizz for around a minute until smooth, then add the melted chocolate and pulse for around 30 seconds.

4. Spoon the mixture into a lined 20cm (8in) square baking tray or mould and bake for 20 minutes. Leave to cool while you prepare the frosting.

5. Place the frosting ingredients in a food processor and whizz for around 5 minutes, stopping to scrape any pieces of avocado down the sides if needed. Spread onto the brownies and slice.

6. Store in an airtight container in the fridge for up to 3 days or freeze for up to 2 months.

## For the brownies

105g (⅔ cup) chocolate chunks (vegan store-bought or make your own, see page 21)
1 ripe avocado
2 flax eggs
160g (½ cup) pure maple syrup
75g (¾ cup) cacao powder
50g (½ cup) ground almonds (sub with ground oats to make nut-free)
pinch of Himalayan salt

## For the frosting

1 ripe avocado
3 tablespoons cacao powder
3 tablespoons pure maple syrup
1 teaspoon vanilla extract
pinch of Himalayan salt

# CARAMEL BANOFFEE BROWNIES

I love jokes more than anyone in the entire world (I think) and I always have done. When I was little, we passed my Grandpa's car on a snow day and I insisted that my Dad write my favourite joke on the frosty windscreen: 'Why do cows have bells? Because their horns don't work.' I still like that one. Anyway, this next question may sound like a joke but for once I am deadly serious. What do you get if you cross a banoffee pie with a brownie? You get caramel banoffee brownie heaven; all the rich fudgy chocolateyness of a brownie, with sweet banana chunks and gooey caramel all thrown in. These brownies are no joke; they're the real deal. ✻ *makes a 20cm (8in) square tray-full*

## For the brownies

100g (1 cup) cacao powder
100g (½ cup) coconut oil
150g (1 cup) Medjool dates
6 tablespoons pure maple syrup
35g (⅓ cup) ground almonds
120g (½ cup) cashew butter
pinch of Himalayan salt
125ml (½ cup) water
2 ripe bananas, sliced

## For the caramel frosting

75g (½ cup) Medjool dates
120g (½ cup) cashew butter
3 tablespoons coconut oil, melted
80ml (⅓ cup) water
pinch of Himalayan salt

1. Preheat your oven to 160°C/gas mark 3.

2. Pop all the ingredients for the brownies except the bananas into a food processor and blend for a couple of minutes until a smooth and sticky batter forms. If it's too sticky (ie it forms a big ball), just add in a little more water a tablespoon at a time until you get the desired consistency.

3. Spoon half the batter into a lined 20cm (8in) square baking tray or mould and press down with a spoon to make sure it's all nice and even, then lay the banana slices on top and finally spoon the remaining half of the batter in, again pressing down to make sure it's evenly spread.

4. Place in the oven and bake for 30 minutes, then leave for another half an hour to cool (as the brownies will continue to cook after they are taken out of the oven).

5. For the caramel frosting, place the ingredients in a food processor and whizz for about 5 minutes until a warm, sticky, smooth caramel mixture forms. Dollop this on top of the brownies, then cut into squares and dig in!

# STICKY PECAN CHOCOLATE COOKIE SLICES

I don't think we spend enough time talking about pecans. They're not just for autumn; they're so luxurious and decadent and they work amazingly in both sweet and savoury dishes all year round. For me, they conjure up *Little House on the Prairie*-esque images, wholesome and cosy, in a life where a warm baked dessert solves pretty much every problem.

I've made pecan pies in all sorts of variations, but these slices are nothing short of double pecan heaven. A buttery, crumbly cookie base topped with a gooey, nutty chocolatey fudgy topping: the kind of indulgence that only pecans can bring to the table.

*✳ makes a 20cm (8in) square tray-full*

*For the base*
100g (1 cup) pecans
100g (1 cup) porridge oats
100g (½ cup) coconut oil, softened
160g (½ cup) pure maple syrup

*For the pecan chocolate fudge layer*
115g (¾ cup) Medjool dates
125ml (½ cup) full-fat coconut milk
4 tablespoons cacao powder
4 tablespoons pure maple syrup
5 tablespoons coconut oil
pinch of Himalayan salt
150g (1½ cups) pecans

1. Preheat your oven to 180°C/gas mark 4.

2. Place the ingredients for the base in a food processor and blend until they form a sticky mixture, then press this into a lined 20cm (8in) square baking tin or tray and bake for 10 minutes.

3. Blend the dates and coconut milk in a food processor until smooth, then place this mixture along with the cacao powder, maple syrup, coconut oil and salt in a saucepan and heat on a medium heat for around 10 minutes, stirring gently, until it begins to thicken.

4. Roughly chop 100g (1 cup) of the pecans and stir into the hot fudge mixture. Remove from the heat and pour this over the base. Spread it evenly with a spoon and scatter the remaining pecans on top. Bake for 20 minutes, then leave to cool and once cool, freeze for 4 hours before cutting into slices.

5. Store in the fridge for up to a week or freeze for up to 2 months.

# SPICED CHOCOLATE CINNAMON ROLLS

I love the combination of cinnamon and chocolate. It makes me think of being all warm and snuggled up under a blanket inside on a rainy day, with a hot cup of something sweet and comforting to sip on, and a bingeworthy series of something trashy on the TV. Currently, it's only really the cinnamon and chocolate part that I ever manage to get around to indulging in, but I'm ok with that. These cinnamon rolls are a little more cakey than your traditional versions, but they're so cosy and the creamy frosting on top just works so well. The first time I made these I'd eaten about half the batch before Mr H got home, and then was too full up to eat my dinner. Story of my life, I guess! * *makes 8–10 rolls*

90g (1 cup) ground oats
1 teaspoon baking powder
2 teaspoons ground cinnamon
pinch of Himalayan salt
8 tablespoons coconut yogurt
1 tablespoon coconut sugar

### For the filling
2 tablespoons coconut oil, melted, plus extra for greasing
1½ tablespoons cacao powder
1 tablespoon ground cinnamon
3 tablespoons coconut sugar

### For the creamy glaze (optional)
125ml (½ cup) coconut yogurt
6 tablespoons oat milk
1 teaspoon ground cinnamon
1 tablespoon coconut sugar
1 teaspoon vanilla extract

1. Preheat your oven to 180°C/gas mark 4.

2. Add the oats, baking powder, cinnamon, coconut sugar and salt to a bowl and mix together, then stir in the coconut yogurt.

3. Knead the dough until you can make it into a ball (it should still be a little sticky), then lightly flour a work surface and roll out the dough into a rectangle about 10cm wide and 5mm (0.2in) thick.

4. Brush half of the melted coconut oil onto the dough, then in a small bowl mix together the cacao powder, cinnamon and coconut sugar and sprinkle this onto the dough.

5. Roll the dough up lengthways into a log then, using a sharp knife, slice it into rolls around 4cm thick. Place the rolls sideways into a small baking dish greased with coconut oil, brush the rest of the coconut oil on top, then bake for 20 minutes or until golden on top.

6. To make the glaze, simply combine the ingredients together in a bowl and spoon it on top of the rolls once they have cooled a little, then dig in!

## Top tip
Make sure your blender is completely dry before grinding the oats and blend for as long as it takes to form a fine flour. If it is too grainy, it will affect the texture of the rolls.

# WHITE CHOCOLATE AND RASPBERRY BLONDIES

I think it's something about the sweetness of white chocolate that works so well with the tartness of raspberries, and in these blondies the flavours come together so nicely. I used to sell these brownies at my little market stall in Hampstead back in the day, and they went down such a treat. My Dad was always my first customer and he'd put some money in my money box so that whilst he helped me on my stall (which he did simply because he enjoyed it), he could help himself to my stock. And never a week went by where a blondie wasn't on his hit list.

These blondies are gooey in the middle and golden on top, with white chocolate chunks and raspberries making them next-level delicious. I like to make my own white chocolate for the chunks, but you can use ready-made white chocolate too.

✳ *makes a 20cm (8in) square tray-full*

170g (1⅔ cups) ground almonds
40g (⅓ cup) buckwheat flour
160g (⅔ cup) peanut butter
125ml (½ cup) almond milk
220g (⅔ cup) pure maple syrup
1 teaspoon vanilla extract
2 tablespoons coconut oil
70g (½ cup) white chocolate chunks
　　(see below or use any vegan white
　　chocolate broken into chunks)
60g (½ cups) raspberries (fresh or frozen)

*For the white chocolate chunks*
75g (⅓ cup) cacao butter
2 tablespoons pure maple syrup
1 tablespoon peanut butter
½ teaspoon vanilla extract

1. Preheat your oven to 180°C/gas mark 4.

2. Make the white chocolate in advance by melting the cacao butter in a bowl over a saucepan half-full of water on a low heat, making sure the bowl is not touching the water, then remove from the heat and stir in the other ingredients until well combined. Pour the mixture into bar-shaped moulds or an ice-cube tray and place in the fridge to set.

3. Pop the ground almonds and buckwheat flour in a bowl and mix well.

4. In a separate bowl, stir together the peanut butter, almond milk, maple syrup and vanilla, then cream in the coconut oil (melt it a little bit if it's very hard). Pour this mixture into the dry ingredients and mix well. Finally, chop the chocolate into chunks and stir these in, along with the raspberries.

5. Spoon the mixture into a 20cm (8in) square baking tin or mould, then bake for 25 minutes. Allow to cool before cutting into delicious squares!

# CHOCOLATE-CHIP SCONES

Growing up, we did a lot of summer holidays down in Cornwall, which in turn meant we ate a lot of scones (with clotted cream and jam, of course). My Mum now lives down there, and a scone, a pasty and a blustery beach walk are a rite of passage when we visit. My only gripe though is when people put raisins in scones. I love raisins, don't get me wrong, but in scones, I am not a fan. So, I've replaced them with chocolate chips because if in doubt, chocolate. They're the perfect teatime treat, best enjoyed with a cuppa somewhere cosy. I believe that's what's known as '*hygge*'.

✳ *makes around 10 scones*

250ml (1 cup) oat milk, plus extra for brushing
1 tablespoon apple cider vinegar
6 tablespoons coconut oil, softened
200g (2 cups) ground almonds
120g (1 cup) buckwheat flour
90g (1 cup) ground oats
pinch of Himalayan salt
1 tablespoon pure maple syrup
70g (½ cup) chocolate chunks (vegan
    store-bought or make your own, see page 21)
strawberry jam and vegan cream, to serve

1. Preheat your oven to 200°C/gas mark 6.

2. Combine the oat milk and vinegar in a bowl and stir gently to form a buttermilk, then set aside.

3. In a mixing bowl, soften the coconut oil with your hands, then add in the almonds, buckwheat flour, ground oats and salt and rub together with the coconut oil. Pour in the maple syrup and the buttermilk mixture and knead into a dough, then fold in the chocolate chunks.

4. Shape the dough into discs 2–3cm high and place on a lined baking tray. Brush a little oat milk on top of the scones and bake for 12 minutes or until golden on top.

5. Allow to cool slightly before serving with jam and vegan cream.

# KITCHEN SINK CHOCOLATE TIFFIN

NUT-FREE option

Did you know that a tiffin is basically a rocky road with chocolate on top? Which in my opinion makes it even better. Apparently, it was invented in Scotland, which is where my Grandpa was born, so maybe that's why I feel such a connection to it. 'Tiffing' means 'to take a little drink' in British slang, and a little cup of tea is the perfect accompaniment to a slice of this. It's so easy to make and a great way to use up any leftover biscuits as well as any nuts and dried fruit you might have in your kitchen cupboards! Who knew zero waste could taste so delicious. * *makes 1 loaf*

### For the base
100g (½ cup) coconut oil
5 tablespoons cacao powder
5 tablespoons pure maple syrup
5 tablespoons peanut butter (or
    a seed butter to make it nut-free)
pinch of Himalayan salt
100g (1 cup) crushed biscuits
75g (½ cup) nuts of choice (or
    seeds to make it nut-free)
80g (⅓ cup) dried fruit of choice

### For the topping
75g (⅓ cup) cacao butter
4 tablespoons cacao powder
3 tablespoons pure maple syrup

1. Melt the coconut oil in a bowl over a saucepan half-full of water on a low heat, making sure the bowl is not touching the water, then remove from the heat and stir in the cacao powder, maple syrup, peanut butter and salt until well mixed.

2. Stir in the biscuits, nuts and dried fruit, then transfer the mixture to a lined baking loaf tin and place in the fridge for half an hour to set.

3. For the topping, melt the cacao butter in a bowl as before, then stir in the other ingredients and pour on top of the base. Place in the fridge for another 20 minutes to set, then slice up and enjoy.

4. Store in an airtight container in the fridge for up to a week or freeze for up to 2 months.

### Top tip
You can use coconut oil instead of cacao butter for the topping layer. I like the harder chocolate texture that the cacao butter provides, but both are delicious!

# BEST-OF-BOTH-WORLDS BROOKIES

I was always confused when I was younger and someone spoke about 'the best of both worlds'. Where was this other world? I knew of only one, and after checking all my cupboards for secret Narnia-like entrances to the other one, I admitted defeat and asked what it actually meant.

I was reminded of these sorts of funny phrases again recently when I told my daughter something wasn't 'the end of the world' and she looked at me like I was a total weirdo. The jury's still out on that one. But these brookies are the perfect example of the best of both worlds: all the gooey 'chocolateyness' of a brownie, topped with crumbly vanilla cookie in every bite.

*✳ makes a 20cm (8in) square tray-full*

*For the brownies*
100g (1 cup) cacao powder
150g (1 cup) Medjool dates
125ml (½ cup) oat milk
220g (⅔ cup) pure maple syrup
120g (½ cup) cashew butter
50g (½ cup) ground almonds
70g (1/3 cup) coconut oil

*For the cookies*
100g (1 cup) porridge oats
100g (1 cup) ground almonds
pinch of Himalayan salt
120g (½ cup) cashew butter
160g (½ cup) pure maple syrup
70g (⅓ cup) coconut oil, melted
70g (½ cup) chocolate chunks (vegan store-bought or make your own, see page 21)

1. Preheat your oven to 150°C/gas mark 2.

2. For the brownies, simply combine the ingredients in a food processor and whizz for around a minute or so until you have a smooth, gooey batter. Spoon this into a lined 20cm (8in) square baking tin, foil tray or silicone mould.

3. To make the cookies, blitz the oats in a food processor for about a minute until they become a flour, then add them to a mixing bowl and stir in the ground almonds and salt.

4. Cream in the cashew butter, maple syrup and coconut oil, mixing well until you have a sticky cookie dough. Lastly, throw in the chocolate chips and mix them in well, then spoon the batter on top of the brownie layer.

5. Bake for 60 minutes, then leave to cool completely before cutting into squares.

6. Store in the fridge for up to a week or in the freezer in an airtight container for up to two months.

# TRIPLE-CHOC MILLIONAIRE SHORTBREAD

What's better than being a millionaire? Being a triple millionaire. Because surely if 'three is a magic number' then one million threes means a whole lot of magic. Simple maths aside, these were one of my favourite treats growing up, but if I had to give any feedback it would be that chocolate in only one-third of the layers wasn't the kind of ratio I was hoping for. So, I've created these, where no layer is left unchocofied. Triple the chocolate = triple the deliciousness. Now that's my kind of equation.

✳ *makes a 20cm (8in) square tray-full*

### For the base
75g (¾ cup) ground almonds
90g (1 cup) ground oats
25g (¼ cup) cacao powder
60g (⅓ cup) coconut sugar
3 tablespoons coconut oil, melted
4 tablespoons peanut butter

### For the caramel
2 batches of my chocolate caramel (see page 22)

### For the chocolate
100g (½ cup) coconut oil
45g (¼ cup) coconut sugar
25g (¼ cup) cacao powder
2 tablespoons peanut butter
pinch of Himalayan salt

1. Preheat your oven to 180°C/gas mark 4.

2. Mix the ground almonds, ground oats, cacao powder and coconut sugar in a bowl, then stir in the coconut oil and peanut butter.

3. With your hands, knead this into a biscuit dough and evenly press it down over the base of a lined 20cm (8in) square baking tin or tray. Bake for 10 minutes, then leave to cool.

4. Make the caramel as per the instructions on page 22, then spread this over the biscuit base and freeze for an hour.

5. For the chocolate, melt the coconut oil in a bowl over a saucepan half-full of water on a low heat, then remove from the heat and stir in the other ingredients. Pour this on top of the caramel layer and place in the fridge for half an hour to set, before cutting into slices.

6. Store in the fridge for up to 2 weeks or freeze for up to 2 months.

# PISTACHIO AND CHOCOLATE FUDGE FLAPJACKS

Mr H loves my original chocolate fudge flapjacks. He thinks they are one of my finest recipes and by the rate he eats them, I think he really means it. He loves chocolate as much as I do, but a couple of years ago he surprised me at an ice-cream stall by asking for pistachio. I mean he did get two scoops and the other was chocolate, but these are now his two go-to scoop flavours. So, this recipe is dedicated to my amazing husband; fudgy flapjacks, with a bit of chocolate and a bit of pistachio too.

*makes a 20cm (8in) square tray-full*

## Top tip

Pistachios normally come with a little brown skin still on. If you'd prefer your fudge to be greener in colour, remove this after roasting by rubbing them in between a cloth once cooled.

### For the homemade pistachio butter
200g (1½ cups) shelled pistachios

### For the base
5 tablespoons coconut oil
3 tablespoons pistachio butter
80g (¼ cup) pure maple syrup
150g (1½ cups) jumbo oats
30g (¼ cup) cacao nibs
40g (¼ cup) shelled and chopped pistachios

### For the fudge
50g (¼ cup) coconut oil
80g (⅓ cup) pistachio butter
2 tablespoons pure maple syrup
pinch of Himalayan salt
2 tablespoons cacao powder

1. Preheat your oven to 165°C/gas mark 3.

2. To make the pistachio butter, roast the pistachios for 10 minutes, then leave to cool before blending them in a high-speed blender, stopping at intervals to scrape down the mixture, until it is runny in texture. Set aside while you make the base.

3. Melt the coconut oil for the base in a saucepan before stirring in the pistachio butter and maple syrup and removing from the heat. Fold in the oats, cacao nibs and pistachios, and spoon into a lined 20cm (8in) square baking tin or tray and press down evenly. Place in the freezer while you make the fudge.

4. Melt the coconut oil for the fudge in a saucepan, then stir in all the other ingredients except the cacao powder and remove from the heat.

5. Transfer half of the fudge mixture into a bowl and stir in the cacao powder. Spoon alternating spoonfuls of the plain pistachio and chocolate pistachio mixture on top of the base, then use a skewer or chopstick and gently swirl around to make marble patterns.

6. Place in the fridge for 2 hours to set, then cut into slices and store in an airtight container in the fridge for up to a week or freeze for up to 2 months.

# MAGIC COOKIE BARS

Magic cookie bars are exactly what they say on the tin. They are typically made with a crumbly crust, topped with layers of butterscotch, coconut, nuts and of course chocolate. But why are they magic? Well firstly they'll disappear before your very eyes and secondly there must be some sort of sorcery to make something this scrumptious. These bars have seven layers, which adds to their mysticism as in Kabbalah, seven is the number of magic and spiritual illumination. So if you're looking for enlightenment or you're just in the market for a tasty treat, these are just the ticket!

* *makes a 20cm (8in) square tray-full*

125g (1¼ cups) porridge oats
25g (¼ cup) cacao powder
1 tablespoon vanilla extract
110g (⅓ cup) plus 3 tablespoons pure maple syrup
310ml (1¼ cups) full-fat coconut milk
50g (½ cup) desiccated coconut
110g (¾ cup) chopped pecans and walnuts
    (or seeds to make it nut-free)
105g (¾ cup) chocolate chunks (vegan
    store-bought or make your own, see page 21)

1. Preheat your oven to 180°C/gas mark 4.

2. Place the oats, cacao powder, vanilla extract and maple syrup in a food processor and blend until sticky and combined. Press this into a lined 20cm (8in) square baking tin or mould and bake for 10 minutes, then leave to cool.

3. Pour the coconut milk on top of the baked crust. Sprinkle the coconut on top, then the nuts and finally the chocolate chunks.

4. Bake for another 40 minutes, then leave to cool in the fridge before slicing.

5. Store in an airtight container in the fridge for up to 2 weeks or freeze for up to 2 months.

# MOVIE NIGHT SWEET-AND-SALTY POPCORN FUDGE BARS

I've loved films and going to the cinema for as long as I can remember, but indecisive old me was always in such a quandary over movie-viewing snacks. I wanted chocolate but I also wanted popcorn. And if I got popcorn, did I go for sweet or salty? I'd often get a small bag of pick 'n' mix and ask the person manning the popcorn stand to put a bit of both flavours in.

These bars incorporate all my favourite things together: the sweet and the salty, the popcorn and the chocolate. They are the perfect snack for a movie night on the sofa, and whilst these days I often don't get to pick the film, at least I get to pick the snacks!

*∗ makes a 20cm (8in) square tray-full*

### For the bars
50g (¼ cup) popcorn kernels
3 tablespoons light olive oil
pinch of Himalayan salt
100g (½ cup) coconut oil
120g (½ cup) peanut butter
6 tablespoons pure maple syrup

### For the chocolate fudge
100g (½ cup) coconut oil
6 tablespoons peanut butter
6 tablespoons cacao powder
6 tablespoons maple syrup
pinch of Himalayan salt

1. To make the bars, pop the popcorn in a pan by adding the olive oil to a large saucepan with a lid and leaving it to heat on a medium to high heat with five of the popcorn kernels. Once these have popped, the oil is hot enough.

2. Remove from the heat for 30 seconds, add in the rest of the kernels, then place the lid back on and pop back onto the heat. Wait until there are 2–3 seconds between pops and remove from the heat.

3. Pour the popcorn into a large bowl, removing any unpopped kernels, add in the salt and toss.

4. In a heatproof bowl, melt the coconut oil over a saucepan half-full of water on a medium heat, making sure the bowl is not touching the water, then remove from the heat once melted and stir in the peanut butter and maple syrup.

5. Pour this mixture into the bowl with the popcorn and stir well. Place the popcorn mixture in a lined 20cm (8in) square baking tin or mould, then pop in the freezer to set for 15 minutes.

6. To make the fudge on top, melt the coconut oil as above, then stir in the other ingredients until all is well combined. Pour this on top of the popcorn mixture and place in the fridge for an hour to set (or the freezer for 30 minutes if you are pushed for time/desperate to eat them).

7. Cut into slices and store in the fridge for up to 2 weeks or freeze for up to 2 months.

Puddings and ice cream go together like yin and yang, salt and pepper or gin and tonic. Give me a warm gooey pudding and some cold ice cream and I'm in heaven. This chapter is the best of both; you might say I've saved the best for last as this chapter really is the jewel in this book's crown.

Many of these desserts take me back to Friday night dinners with my family where there would always be something good for dessert, and ice cream, too. The house would smell so amazing with the scent of something baking in the oven that I'd spend the whole meal counting down until it was time for pudding.

# Chapter 8

*

# PUDDINGS &
# ICE CREAMS

# CHEAT'S CHOCOLATE FONDANTS

If Goldilocks had broken into my house, she'd have found three chocolate fondants, and every one of them would have been just right. There would have been no messing around with too hot or too cold, too big or too small; she'd have scoffed the lot and probably got out long before the three bears came home and caught her breaking and entering on their Ring doorbell.

These chocolate fondants are so easy to make, three bears could make them, no problem. I like to pop some extra chocolate in the middle as a little cheat's way of ensuring that the centre is perfectly molten, gooey and oh so indulgent. My three little bears can't get enough of them. ✱ *makes 3 fondants*

### For the cheat's centres
3 tablespoons coconut oil
3 tablespoons cacao powder
2 tablespoons pure maple syrup

### For the fondants
coconut oil, for greasing
80ml (⅓ cup) oat milk
1 teaspoon apple cider vinegar
5 tablespoons cacao powder, plus extra for dusting
30g (⅓ cup) ground oats
60g (⅓ cup) coconut sugar
3 tablespoons pure maple syrup

1.  Melt the coconut oil and stir in the cacao powder and maple syrup, then spoon this into an ice-cube tray equally between three cubes and place in the freezer.

2.  Grease three ramekins with coconut oil and dust with cacao powder.

3.  Preheat your oven to 190°C/gas mark 5.

4.  In a bowl, mix together the oat milk and vinegar, then add in the other ingredients and whisk until smooth.

5.  Spoon half the mixture into the ramekins, then place a chocolate cube into the middle of each and cover with the remaining mixture.

6.  Bake for 20 minutes, then allow to cool for 5 minutes before serving. Best consumed warm, before Goldilocks gets a whiff of them.

# CHOCO-BANANA CRUMBLE

When I was little we used to have Friday night dinner with my grandparents every week, as is tradition. It was the only meal of the week where we'd have three courses, and dessert was usually a crumble, always served with ice cream. It wasn't unusual for me to be 'too full up' to help with the dishes afterwards. When I met Mr H it transpired that his rather more British family tradition was to have a family lunch every Sunday, also with a crumble for dessert. So, now we get the best of both worlds: double crumble, with Saturday as a day off in between. This version mixes it up a little by using bananas and chocolate, and it always goes down a treat! *serves 4*

### For the crumble topping
35g (⅓ cup) porridge oats
30g (¼ cup) chopped pecans
25g (¼ cup) cacao powder
4 tablespoons coconut sugar
2 tablespoons coconut oil
2 tablespoons peanut butter
pinch of Himalayan salt

### For the crumble filling
2 large bananas, sliced
2 tablespoons coconut sugar

1. Preheat your oven to 180°C/gas mark 4.

2. For the crumble topping, blitz the oats in a blender for 30 seconds to break them down a little, then add them to a bowl with the other ingredients and stir it all together well.

3. Place the sliced bananas evenly on the base of an oven dish, then sprinkle them with the coconut sugar.

4. Spoon the topping evenly over the bananas, then bake for 25 minutes.

5. Serve with ice cream!

# CHOCOLATE PEAR POKE PUDDING

My kids love this one; they get a chopstick each to poke holes in the pudding before the sauce goes on and it's like part sensory play, part science experiment. The dark chocolate is mellowed out by sweet juicy pears, and the sauce that soaks through the holes.
* *serves 4–6*

3 ripe medium pears, peeled, cored and halved
50g (½ cup) ground almonds
30g (¼ cup) buckwheat flour
50g (½ cup) cacao powder
85g (½ cup) coconut sugar
50g (¼ cup) coconut oil, melted, plus extra for greasing
80g (⅓ cup) almond butter
125ml (½ cup) water
2 flax eggs (2 tablespoons ground flaxseed left in 6 tablespoons water for 5 minutes to thicken)

### For the chocolate sauce
60ml (¼ cup) full-fat coconut milk
45g (¼ cup) coconut sugar
105g (¾ cup) chocolate chunks (vegan store-bought or make your own, see page 21)
60ml (¼ cup) boiling water

1. Preheat your oven to 200°C/gas mark 6 and grease a 20cm (8in) square baking tin or tray with coconut oil. Arrange the pears evenly on the tray.

2. Put the dry ingredients in a bowl and mix well, before stirring in the coconut oil, almond butter, water and flax eggs. Spoon this over the pears and bake for 25 minutes, then leave to cool.

3. For the sauce, bring the coconut milk to the boil in a saucepan. Reduce the heat and stir in the coconut sugar until dissolved. Place the chocolate chunks in a separate bowl and pour the boiling water on top. Cover and leave for five minutes, then stir together. Pour the mixture into the saucepan and gently stir. With a chopstick, poke little holes all over the pudding, then pour the sauce on top. Serve up!

# STICKY CHOCCY PUDDING

NUT-FREE

My only issue with sticky toffee pudding is the lack of chocolate involved. I used to solve this with chocolate ice cream on the side to get my fix, but then I realised I had the power vested in me to take matters into my own hands and make a solution once and for all. So, I 'chocofied' it. Spoiler alert: it was epic, hence why it's made it onto these very pages. It's one of those things you need to eat straight out of the oven, potentially even straight from the dish. I won't judge, it's very easily done! * *serves 6–8*

250ml (1 cup) oat milk
300g (2 cups) Medjool dates
1 teaspoon apple cider vinegar
85g (½ cup) coconut sugar
100g (½ cup) coconut oil
100g (1 cup) cacao powder
pinch of Himalayan salt

### For the toffee sauce
130g (¾ cup) coconut sugar
250ml (1 cup) full-fat coconut milk
pinch of Himalayan salt

1. Preheat your oven to 190°C/gas mark 5. Place the oat milk and the dates in a saucepan on a low heat and heat for 10 minutes, stirring gently, before stirring in the apple cider vinegar.

2. Pour these into a food processor along with the other pudding ingredients and blend for 2 to 3 minutes until smooth. Spoon the mixture into a lined 20cm (8in) square baking tin or tray and bake for 25 minutes.

3. While this is cooking, add the sauce ingredients to a saucepan and bring to a boil, stirring gently, then leave to simmer for 20 minutes, stirring occasionally.

4. Slice and serve the pudding immediately, with the sauce poured on top.

# CHOC-CHIP COOKIE SKILLET

Mr H and I very nearly fell out when he once told me he'd been for a work lunch and had what he described as 'the best dessert in London'. I was so cross I didn't make him any pudding for a week. I went through all the stages: denial, self-doubt, anger, before deciding I had to know what this dessert was so I could up my game.

He confessed: it was a cookie skillet, crunchy on top but gooey in the middle. He said it was a one-time thing and that he still loved my desserts, but I knew I had to make sure he didn't stray again. My skillet turned up the next day, and this recipe was born. He says he's not been back to that restaurant since. ✶ *fills a 25cm (10in) cast-iron skillet*

100g (½ cup) coconut oil, melted, plus extra for greasing
150g (1½ cups) ground almonds
135g (1½ cups) ground oats
1½ teaspoons bicarbonate of soda
200g (1¾ cups) coconut sugar
pinch of Himalayan salt
120g (½ cup) cashew butter
125ml (½ cup) plus 2 tablespoons almond milk
1 teaspoon vanilla extract
1 tablespoon flaxseed
175g (1¼ cups) chocolate chunks (vegan store-bought or make your own, see page 21)

1. Preheat your oven to 160°C/gas mark 3 then grease a 25cm (10in) cast-iron skillet with coconut oil.

2. Stir together the ground almonds, ground oats, bicarbonate of soda, coconut sugar and salt in a bowl, then set aside.

3. In another bowl, mix together the coconut oil, cashew butter, almond milk, vanilla extract and flaxseeds, stirring together until combined.

4. Add the dry ingredients to the wet and continue stirring, then lastly add the chocolate chunks.

5. Transfer the mixture into the skillet, making sure it is spread evenly. Bake for 35 minutes, then allow to cool briefly before digging in!

# SELF-SAUCING CHOCOLATE PUDDING

Your car might be able to self-drive, your oven might be able to self-clean, but can your pudding self-sauce? This dessert is like the Tesla of all bakes: it's very smooth, requires very little human input and you'll be the envy of your neighbours when you make it. It's also possibly the most delicious experiment you could ever do – you make the pudding, sprinkle some cacao and coconut sugar on top and then add boiling water, which seems a little bizarre but trust me on this one. Like all jazzy new technology, once you've given it a try, you'll never know how you lived without it! * *serves 4–6*

*For the pudding*
100g (1 cup) porridge oats
25g (¼ cup) cacao powder
85g (½ cup) coconut sugar
pinch of Himalayan salt
50g (¼ cup) coconut oil
80g (¼ cup) pure maple syrup
60ml (¼ cup) oat milk

*For the sauce*
3 tablespoons coconut sugar
2 tablespoons cacao powder
125ml (½ cup) boiling water

1. Preheat your oven to 180°C/gas mark 4.

2. In a food processor or blender, whizz the oats for around a minute until they become a flour, then combine this in a bowl with the cacao powder, coconut sugar and salt, stirring well.

3. In a saucepan, melt the coconut oil on a low heat and stir in the maple syrup and oat milk, then pour this into the dry ingredients and mix gently.

4. Pour the mixture into an ovenproof dish (mine is 18cm x 13cm) and set aside.

5. Mix together the coconut sugar and cacao powder for the sauce and sprinkle it over the mixture. Pour the boiling water on top and place in the oven for 25 minutes or until it looks cooked in the middle.

6. Serve straight away, and level up with extra chocolate sauce (see page 23) or ice cream!

# CHOC-CHUNK BREAD AND BUTTER PUDDING

There are a few lovely bakeries near our house, so sometimes if we're having a chilled-out day and fancy a little potter, we'll wander down to the high street and grab a fresh loaf. The thing with fresh bread though is that without any preservatives, it can quite often be a little hard if you don't get through it all in a day or two. If it's too hard to eat, then I'll make it into croutons or, my personal favourite, bread and butter pudding. It's possibly the most nostalgic dessert out there in my opinion, and this one has the most delicious chocolatey twist.

\* *serves 6–8*

3 tablespoons coconut oil, softened
4 thick slices of bread, with the crusts cut off
70g (½ cup) chocolate chunks (vegan store-bought or make your own, see page 21)
65g (½ cup) cashews, soaked in hot water for at least 4 hours
2 tablespoons cacao powder
80g (¼ cup) pure maple syrup
500ml (2 cups) almond milk
1 tablespoon ground flaxseed
1 teaspoon vanilla extract
1 teaspoon ground cinnamon

1.  Preheat your oven to 180°C/gas mark 4.

2.  Spread the softened coconut oil onto your bread and cut the slices into quarters, then place them in a 25cm x 18cm (10in x 7in) oven dish so that the bottom is covered. Sprinkle on the chocolate chunks.

3.  Blend the cashews, cacao powder, maple syrup, almond milk, flaxseed, vanilla extract and cinnamon in a blender until it becomes a smooth liquid, then evenly pour this on top of the bread mixture.

4.  Bake in the oven for 25 minutes, allowing to cool briefly before serving.

# CHOCOLATE PB TRIFLE JARS

It might surprise you to know this, but when I was little, trifle was the one dessert I didn't love. I loved the idea of it: fruit good, custard good, sponge good (and ten bonus points if you get the *Friends* reference there), but I just don't think it was chocolatey enough for me. This version, however, most definitely is. It combines two of my favourite things – chocolate and peanut butter. I love taking these jars on picnics or days out, and they're a great way to use up any leftover brownies, not that that's often required in our house!

*\* makes 4 small jars*

120g (½ cup) runny peanut butter (or a nut-free butter)
500ml (2 cups) almond or coconut yogurt
3 tablespoons pure maple syrup
4 brownies, crumbled into crumbs (2 cups)
70g (½ cup) chocolate chunks (vegan store-bought or make your own, see page 21)- or cacao nibs

*For the whipped cream*
120g (½ cup) coconut cream (the hard part of coconut milk), refrigerated
1 teaspoon vanilla extract

*Optional toppings*
peanut butter
cacao nibs

1. In a bowl, mix together the peanut butter, yogurt and maple syrup.

2. Spoon 2 tablespoons of brownie crumbs into 4 small jars as the base, followed by 4 tablespoons of peanut butter mixture, then a tablespoon of chocolate chunks. Repeat this until you have used up all the ingredients.

3. Put the coconut cream in a stand or hand mixer and whip until fluffy, then gently stir in the vanilla and pipe or spoon this on top of the peanut mixture.

4. Drizzle with peanut butter and sprinkle with cacao nibs to serve. Store in the fridge for up to 3 days.

## Top tip
If you don't have a stand mixer, you can always give the cream a quick whisk by hand. It won't be quite as fluffy, but it will still be delicious!

# WHITE CHOCOLATE CARAMEL FUDGESICLE BARS

**NUT-FREE** *option*

'Good things come to those who wait.' It's one of those annoying phrases that your parents tell you when you're young, impatient and don't have the time to listen to advice from your elders. Well, I have to say, I've waited and I've waited for all sorts of things, and a lot of the time it rings true. Especially when, like me, none of your children ever seem to want to be born before their due date. I'm quite a seasoned 'waiter' now, which is ironic because often at home I feel like a waitress. So, whilst you'll have to wait overnight for these to set before you can add the final layers, I promise you, they are worth said wait. These fudgesicles are so sweet and light, with a layer of caramel and all covered in delicious white chocolate. ✳ *makes 6 bars*

### For the bars

180ml (¾ cup) oat milk
120g (½ cup) coconut cream (the hard part of coconut milk), refrigerated
45g (¼ cup) coconut sugar
1 teaspoon vanilla extract

### For the caramel

2 tablespoons coconut sugar
60g (¼ cup) coconut cream, like above

### For the white chocolate

115g (½ cup) cacao butter
2 tablespoons pure maple syrup
1 tablespoon cashew butter (or
   tahini to make nut-free)
½ teaspoon vanilla extract

1. For the bars, whisk together all the ingredients except the vanilla in a saucepan over a medium heat and bring it to a boil. Then simmer on a medium heat for around 10 minutes until the sugar has dissolved and the mixture has thickened slightly. Remove from the heat, stir in the vanilla and leave to cool for 10 minutes. Pour this into lolly moulds and freeze overnight.

2. Put the caramel ingredients in a bowl, stir well and bring to a boil, then simmer on a low heat for 30 minutes. Leave to cool, then spoon the caramel onto the top of each of the bars and place them back in the freezer.

3. Melt the cacao butter in a bowl over a saucepan half-full of water, making sure the bowl is not touching the water, and heat on a low heat, stirring gently until melted.

4. Stir in the other white chocolate ingredients, then remove from the heat and dip the bars in this mixture, repeating to create a thicker chocolate layer with the leftover mixture.

5. Store in the freezer for up to 2 months and leave to stand for 5 minutes before serving.

# TIRAMISU

I adore the taste of coffee. One could say that back in my days as an office worker, I was rather addicted to the stuff. I don't chug skinny lattes by the bucket-load like I used to, but once a week or so I'll have a decaff oat flat white and savour every sip. One thing I love about tiramisu, which literally means 'pick me up' in Italian, is that it combines so many elements and different flavours. They're all delicious in their own right but when put together, they make something truly magical. I've given this version a little twist and incorporated a chocolate layer too, because, chocolate. *Bellissima. ✳ makes 4 jars*

### For the cake layer
90g (1 cup) ground oats
85g (½ cup) coconut sugar
100g (1 cup) ground almonds (sub
    for extra oats to make nut-free)
1 tablespoon apple cider vinegar
330ml (1⅓ cups) oat milk
2 tablespoons rapeseed oil
1 teaspoon vanilla extract
60ml (¼ cup) strong brewed coffee
    (add more for a stronger flavour)

### For the chocolate mousse layer
1 medium avocado
115g (¾ cup) Medjool dates
4 tablespoons coconut cream
4 tablespoons cacao powder, plus
extra for dusting

### For the cream layer
240g (1 cup) coconut cream
2 tablespoons pure maple syrup
1 teaspoon vanilla extract

1. Preheat your oven to 180°C/gas mark 4.

2. Put the ground oats, coconut sugar and ground almonds in a bowl and stir well.

3. In another bowl, stir together the apple cider vinegar, oat milk, oil and vanilla.

4. Make a well in the middle of the dry ingredients and pour in the wet ingredients, stirring until well incorporated. Transfer the mixture to two lined loaf tins and bake for 25 minutes or until golden on top and springy to the touch.

5. Once the cakes have cooled, crumble one of them up and place it in the base of four jars, pressing it down evenly. Pour half the coffee mixture over it to soak it.

6. To make the chocolate mousse layer, combine all the ingredients in a food processor or blender and blend until a smooth chocolatey mixture forms. Spoon half of this evenly on top of the coffee-soaked cake layer, then set aside while you make the cream layer.

7. For the cream layer, simply put all the ingredients in a mixing bowl and stir well. Spoon half of this on top of the chocolate mousse layer, then repeat the process with the remaining cake, mousse and cream.

8. Dust a little cacao powder on top and serve.

9. Store in the fridge for up to 3 days or freeze for up to 2 months.

# BANANA 'LOLLIES'

These are wonderfully nostalgic for me. Growing up I hated bananas; I'd go as far as saying I had bananaphobia, much to my brother's delight when he'd chase me around the house pretending to shoot me with one when we were younger. But once my mum made us banana 'lollies' – frozen bananas dipped in chocolate and covered in sprinkles – I just couldn't get enough of them.

These are ever so easy to make and healthier than shop-bought lollies, not to mention tastier! Whenever I have these, it takes me right back, and hopefully my little ones will carry on the same tradition of making them too. ✳ *serves 4*

4 bananas
5 tablespoons cashew butter (or tahini to make nut-free)
50g (¼ cup) coconut oil, melted
2 tablespoons pure maple syrup
3 tablespoons cacao powder

## *Optional toppings*
chopped nuts
desiccated coconut
freeze-dried strawberry pieces

1. Place the bananas in the freezer for 4 hours.

2. Remove from the freezer and, with a knife, spread a tablespoon of the cashew butter evenly onto each of the bananas, then place back in the freezer while you make the chocolate coating.

3. In a bowl, mix together the coconut oil, maple syrup, cacao powder and remaining cashew butter, then dip the bananas in one by one, leaving around an inch uncovered at the end.

4. Hold each banana over the bowl for 30 seconds to allow the chocolate to set, then place on a chopping board covered with baking paper.

5. Repeat the dipping process until the chocolate is finished, then sprinkle on any toppings.

6. Serve immediately or store in the freezer for up to 2 months.

# DOUBLE-CHOCOLATE LOLLIES

'What do cheeky boys get?' I'd ask Buddy when he was two, before tickling him for being cheeky, on a daily basis. 'Ice cream?' he once replied, and we laughed so hard he realised it was funny and that became his go-to answer from then on.

Well, cheeky boys do get ice cream, and one particularly cheeky boy is a huge fan of these lollies. Actually, we all are. Just make sure you eat them quickly because apparently cheeky boys also like taking bites out of other people's ice creams once they've finished their own!
\* *makes 4–6 small ice lollies*

*For the ice cream*
3 tablespoons cacao powder
3 tablespoons hazelnut butter (or other nut butter)
120g (½ cup) coconut cream
1 medium banana
2 tablespoons pure maple syrup

*For the coating*
2 tablespoons coconut oil
2 tablespoons cacao powder
1 tablespoon pure maple syrup
1 tablespoon hazelnut butter (or other nut butter)
4 tablespoons toasted chopped hazelnuts

1. In a food processor, blend the ice-cream ingredients together until mixed. Pour into ice-cream moulds and leave for 4 hours to set.

2. For the coating, melt the coconut oil in a saucepan then stir in the other ingredients.

3. Remove the lollies from their moulds and dunk into the chocolate one by one. Store in the freezer or eat them as soon as the chocolate sets!

# MINTY-CHOC ICE CREAM

I've mentioned already that when I was younger, we'd go to my grandparents for Friday night dinner. Out would come the little dessert trolley, and more often than not a Viennetta would come rolling into view.

Whilst it might be a little bit '90s, some things don't go out of fashion, and ice cream with layers of chocolate is always chic in my opinion (is it really a coincidence that 'chic CEO' is an anagram of 'choc ice'? I think not). Wafer-thin layers of crunchy chocolate alternated with creamy ice cream make this dessert the perfect ending to any meal.
* serves 6–8, fills one loaf tin

*For the ice cream*
**65g (½ cup) cashews, soaked in
   hot water for 2 hours**
**1 x 400ml can of full-fat coconut milk**
**80g (¼ cup) pure maple syrup**
**1 teaspoon peppermint extract**

*For the chocolate*
**100g (½ cup) coconut oil**
**3 tablespoons pure maple syrup**
**4 tablespoons cacao powder**

1. Drain the cashews, place them in a blender with the other ice-cream ingredients and blend for around 5 minutes until smooth. Pour into a bowl and freeze for an hour to allow the ice cream to set a little until it is the texture of thick cream.

2. Melt the coconut oil in a bowl over a saucepan half-full of water on a low heat, making sure the bowl is not touching the water, then remove from the heat and stir in the other ingredients. Leave to cool while you wait for the ic-cream mixture to thicken up.

3. In a lined baking loaf tin or mould, place a thin covering of the ice-cream mixture on the base, spreading it out evenly. Cover this with a thin layer of the chocolate mixture, tilting the tin or mould so that it reaches all four corners. Wait for the chocolate to set (it should be around a minute) then repeat this process of layering until you have used up all the mixture.

4. Place in the freezer for another hour, then remove from the tin or mould and slice to serve, or store in the freezer for up to 2 months and leave to stand for half an hour before serving.

# INDEX

# THANK YOUS

Never in my wildest chocoholic dreams could I have imagined getting to write my very own chocolate recipe book, so this page is dedicated to all the amazing people who helped me make it happen.

To my number one best friend, my husband Richard, once again you've sacrificed your time and your waistline, all whilst working your posterior off, being the best daddy ever and remaining mysteriously calm throughout. Must be something in your wife's cooking.

To my three chocolateers, I am so proud of you all. Azaria, thank you for your enthusiasm, excitement and honesty at every step of the way. You are the perfect little sous chef, and you've insisted on always taste testing everything an extra time (just to be sure).

Buddy, thank you for always wanting to help out (always in the cheekiest and messiest way possible of course). I knew recipes were book-worthy when you'd wait until the coast was clear, pull up a chair to the fridge and help yourself to whatever I was trialling.

And finally Boaz, thank you for hanging out happily in the sling while I created pretty much every recipe in this book. You're possibly the biggest chocoholic of the lot, but given that my milk was probably 90% chocolate during the process of making this book, I guess it's quite literally in your blood.

To my ever-growing family; Brian, Fran, Jonathan, Nicole, Myla, Blake, Stephie, Lara, David, Elia, Luca, Sam, Suzanne, Graham, Matt, Juliet, Ezra and Shiloh – thank you for always happily trying my creations, for helping out with my crazy gang and for all your love and encouragement.

A big shout out also to my amazing friends, thank you for being there for me and for making me feel so loved.

Lastly, a huge thank you to everyone who worked on making this book what I'm pretty sure is my best work to date; Jane and Jen at Graham Maw Christie, the fabulous team at Kyle Books (especially to Samhita), to Jen for once again knocking it out the park with her photography, and Kathy for the most beautiful styling. Thank you also to the lovely Will, Stevie and Max for all your help too and to Helen for design and Kay and Louise for copyediting and proofreading.